Near the Nucerian Gate one family,
like many others in the
town, as the

Their slave, walking beside them, made a vain
attempt to protect himself from the burning
cinders with a fallen roof tile.
Inexorably, the ash continued to pile up,
mounting to the level of house windows,
blocking doorways.
Before long, it had buried even the rooftops.
Terror was extinguished in death;
men and animals,
frozen in their final agony, were transformed
into inanimate matter.

Pompeii, 1961

Almost two thousand years passed before the
archaeologist Amedeo Maiuri found this family.
The slave still held the tile that had failed
to protect him;
the women and children lay hand in hand.
One man, who had clearly fought to the very
end, was still propping himself up on his elbow
in a final effort to rise and
help his loved ones.

CONTENTS

POMPEII
THE DAY A CITY DIED

Robert Etienne

Thames & Hudson

Very rapidly after 24 August AD 79, judging by the available evidence, Pompeii disappeared completely from the face of the inhabited world. On the level earth, grass and vines gradually took possession of land where the town had once stood. Country people soon forgot even its name, referring to the hill that now covered it by the blank term *la cività*, 'the city'.

CHAPTER 1
THE HUNT FOR TREASURE

The death of the city meant not only the destruction of its streets, monuments and houses, but also the death of the inhabitants, struck down in the midst of their everyday activities; their contorted forms were faithfully preserved by the volcanic ash spewed out by Vesuvius.

Chronicle of a famous death: Pliny the Elder

"They decided to go down to the shore, to see at first hand whether it was possible to escape by sea; but they found the waves still wild and dangerous. There a sheet was spread on the ground for my uncle to lie down, and he called repeatedly for cold water, which he drank. Then the flames and smell of sulphur which heralded the approaching fire drove the others to take flight. Aroused, my uncle struggled to his feet, leaning on two slaves, but immediately collapsed. I assume that his breathing was impeded by the dense fumes, which choked his windpipe – for it was constitutionally weak and narrow, and often inflamed. When daylight returned – two days after the last time he had seen it – his body was found intact and uninjured, still fully clothed as in life. He looked more like a sleeper than a dead man."

Pliny the Younger
Letter to Tacitus,
AD 104

Romantic visions inspired by the ruins

If the people who escaped from Pompeii had returned to the scene of the disaster, they would have found no trace of their city, which lay buried beneath the dense layer of ash that had accumulated between 10 a.m. and 1 p.m. on 24 August AD 79. Yet 19th-century painters often chose to evoke the memory of the dead city by combining – as in this painting by Paul Alfred de Curzon, *Dream amid the Ruins of Pompeii* – a typically romanticized vision of the ruins with figures in ancient dress, bewailing the tragic fate of their familiar haunts.

Graffiti reveal that even in the immediate aftermath of the eruption, teams went in to try to recover the most valuable objects from Pompeii, but only in the 18th century was Europe seized with a virtual passion to reveal the lost cities of Pompeii and Herculaneum.

Sack and pillage of a buried city – with the kings' permission

The ruins of Herculaneum had first been discovered in 1594, but it was not until 1709 that serious excavations began. At that time southern Italy was dominated by Austria, and it was the Austrian rulers of Naples who had shafts and tunnels dug in order to plunder statues which were then exported to their Viennese residences. They cared little if, in the process, great holes were smashed in walls covered with paintings. Only one brave voice was raised against this pillage: that of the pope.

Unfortunately, the treasure-seeking was renewed when Charles III of Spain, King of the Two Sicilies, sent Rocco Gioacchino de Alcubierre, a surveying engineer, to supply the Spanish court with statues and precious objects. In 1748 a first excavation site was opened in Pompeii 200 m from the Temple of Fortuna Augusta, close to the Via Stabiana and the Via di Nola (see map on pp. 46-7). This was soon abandoned, however, as Alcubierre decided to transfer his attention to Herculaneum, and it was not until 1754 that excavations at Pompeii were renewed. Only nine years later, thanks to the discovery of an inscription, did *la civtà* regain its true name of Pompeii.

The intelligentsia flocks to Pompeii and Herculaneum – not always for the right reasons

By this time, Europe, alerted by the early visitors to Pompeii, was hungry for details. Scholars began to make the journey to Naples, and the city soon became an important stop on the Grand Tour, which it was fashionable for all aristocratic Englishmen to make. The excavations nearby were later to play an important part in the Neo-classical revival, as artists, architects, furniture-makers and

The village of Resina was built on top of the solidified torrent of mud that put an abrupt end to all life in Herculaneum. Alcubierre's team of 'excavators' (above) fought their way through this wall of mud, which was as hard as petrified lava and 8 m thick, cutting into it to create staircases and ramps, trenches and underground passages.

The mysterious buried city regained its true name thanks to the discovery of an inscription. The Italian artist Giovanni Battista Piranesi immediately introduced the name into one of his engravings.

potters, such as Wedgwood, drew inspiration from Pompeii. Some of Robert Adam's interiors, for example, were based on the frescoed walls and stucco work of Pompeii.

Yet the excavations were far from exemplary; Johann Joachim Winckelmann, the great German archaeologist, made no bones about protesting at the anarchy that ruled there (see p. 146). It was Karl Weber, director of the excavations at Pompeii, who first proposed that, rather than carrying out selective and uncoordinated digs, they should uncover the site systematically, section by section. In this way a tavern, the Tomb of the Istacidii and that of the priestess Mamia were discovered close to the Herculaneum Gate. The imagination of Europe was set ablaze by these discoveries. Weber's successor, the Spaniard Francesco la Vega, discovered the Odeon, or small theatre, in 1764, and then the Temple of Isis, reconstructed after the earthquake of AD 62 by Popidius Celsinus; in 1767 the gladiators' barracks were uncovered. La Vega established the first overall plan of the excavations – indicating an increasingly rational approach to the work – and in spite of the limited workforce at his disposal, the Odeon and the large theatre had been completely cleared by 1789. Yet still the aim was to find precious objects, gold and silver jewelry, and once the purpose of a particular building had been established, its excavation was abandoned.

The road from Pompeii to Herculaneum was the first to be uncovered; beside it was discovered a group of tombs, the necropolis outside the Herculaneum Gate. The mausoleum in the process of being disinterred and restored here (left) is that of the Istacidii; it stands on a low terrace surrounded by a stone balustrade. The vast burial chamber is decorated externally with fluted engaged columns. The solidity of the structure gives some impression of the wealth of this family, who were connected with some of the most important names in Pompeian society.

The Temple of Isis (above right) was discovered in 1765, together with an inscription naming the person responsible for its reconstruction after the earthquake of 5 February AD 62. This watercolour was painted by William Hamilton, English ambassador to the court of Naples, whose life as a diplomat clearly left him sufficient time to visit the excavations.

Between 1770 and 1815 the excavations were given new impetus under the influence of the Neapolitan kings and their wives. Caroline, daughter of Maria Theresa of Austria and wife of the weak and ineffectual Ferdinand I of the Two Sicilies, showed keen interest in the excavations. The Villa of Diomedes was uncovered in 1771, and in 1772 eighteen bodies were discovered in an underground passage; among them was that of a young girl, who inspired the French romantic novelist Théophile Gautier to write the novella *Arria Marcella* in 1852. The fame of Pompeii spread: Goethe visited it in 1787, while Sir William Hamilton, English ambassador to the court of Naples from 1764 to 1800, was a regular and enthusiastic observer at the site.

The writings of Johann Joachim Winckelmann (1717-68), author of a *History of Ancient Art*, helped to spread throughout Europe a taste for the classical world. His critical comments made him unpopular with the Neapolitan court, however. He claimed that Alcubierre knew as much about antiquity as 'the moon knows about lobsters', and, referring to the speed at which work on the excavations was progressing, he wrote: 'At this rate our great-grandchildren will still have plenty of work to do.' Nevertheless, thanks to Hamilton, he was allowed to watch the excavation of what would later be recognized as the gladiators' barracks.

Like many painters of his generation, Jacob Philipp Hackert (1737-1807) visited Italy as part of his Grand Tour, a trip undertaken by young men to study the monuments and art of the classical world. In this painting, which shows the theatre quarter of Pompeii, he reveals the stage excavations had reached by 1799. Thanks to the efforts of the Spaniard La Vega, excavation of the Odeon, or covered theatre (the rectangular building in the foreground, on the left), and of the large theatre (on the right), first discovered in 1764, was finally completed in 1789. The semicircular corridor that gave access to the upper levels of the large theatre is clearly visible. The central courtyard of the gladiators' barracks (behind the Odeon) is surrounded by a colonnade, and on the far right, in the foreground, stand the remains of the Temple of Isis. On the horizon can be seen the outline of the Lattari mountains, where the rich Pompeian landowners grazed their flocks.

In under a decade important buildings are feverishly brought to light

In 1808 Joachim Murat and Queen Caroline, sister of Napoleon I, became rulers of Naples. Passionately interested in archaeology, they delved deep into their own pockets to speed up the excavations. The limits of the town were established; the outer wall was excavated near the Via Consolare,

Pompeii aroused everyone's curiosity. Grisly scenes were staged for early groups of tourists (above), who could also enjoy romantic walks around the Tomb of the Istacidii (above right).

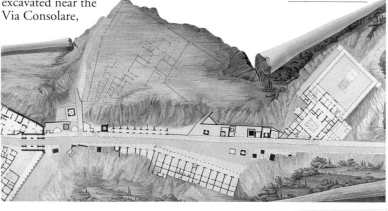

and work continued on the amphitheatre and the basilica. The Napoleonic royal family proved as fascinated by Pompeii as the early Bourbon rulers of Naples had been. But with the return of the old dynasty, work on the excavations slackened. La Vega

died in 1815 and was replaced by Antonio Bonnucci, who in 1818 was working with only thirteen assistants. Yet Pompeii continued to attract the crowned heads of Europe, who were treated to fictitious on-the-spot 'discoveries' of rooms that had been reburied only a few moments before their visit.

In 1823 the forum was excavated, together with the theatre quarter, the remaining portion of the gladiators' barracks, the western wall, the area around the Herculaneum Gate, a long stretch of the Street of Tombs, the amphitheatre, and the houses at the northern end of the Via Stabiana. In 1824 it was the turn of the Temple of Fortuna Augusta and the Forum Baths.

Francis I, king of the Two Sicilies from 1825 to 1830, showed more interest in Pompeii than his brother Ferdinand I had done; a house to the north of the Forum Baths, a bakery and the House of the Tragic Poet were uncovered during his reign. Under his successor Ferdinand II a vast mosaic depicting Alexander the Great at the Battle of Issus was found in the House of the Faun – a find that created intense excitement.

"The strangest thing I saw on my travels was Pompeii, where you feel as if you have been transported back into the ancient world; even if you normally believe only proven facts, here you feel as if, just by being there, you know more about the place than any scholar. What a great pleasure it is to come face to face with antiquity, when one has read so many books about it."

Stendhal
Rome, Naples and Florence, 1817

To the west of the city stands the Herculaneum Gate (visible on the left of the plan opposite). The road to Herculaneum was made up of three lanes – two of which were reserved for pedestrians – and, for the first 200 m outside the city, was bordered by tombs and shops. On the far right is the imposing Villa of Diomedes, the layout of which was reconstructed from details given in an early tax register. The rooms of this suburban villa are arranged around two peristyles. With its extensive garden, established on a lower level, it provides a foretaste of the country villas scattered over the slopes of Vesuvius.

An architect in Pompeii

François Mazois (1783-1826), author of *The Ruins of Pompeii,* trained as an architect under Claude-Nicolas Ledoux and Charles Percier. In 1808 he found himself in Naples, appointed by Murat to direct work on improvements to the city. It was here that he began to restore the ancient monuments of Campania. From 1809 to 1811, he devoted himself to Pompeii: 'Here I am, settled in Pompeii once more, where, in spite of the heat, my riches continue to increase, that is, my collection of finds continues to grow.... I get up very early; at about 9 o'clock the fierce heat of the sun forces me to take a break, so I return to my small room, where I finalize the sketches I have made during the morning. At midday my cook solemnly presents me with a vast plate of macaroni. After I have eaten that, an hour's sleep restores my good humour and enthusiasm, so I set to work again, in my cramped lodgings until 5 o'clock, and then out in the windy open air until sunset. All in all, that means a total of thirteen or fourteen hours' work a day. So you can see I am working hard.'

The poetry of the ruins

The 454 drawings Mazois made, which included views of monuments, plans and studies of individual objects, were engraved and published between 1824 and 1838. The picture on p. 24 reveals the heart of a house in Pompeii, the atrium, whose roof would have been supported by the four columns visible in the centre. On a line with the atrium can be seen the entrance; the stone bench in front of the house, on which a soldier is resting, is where visitors and clients would have waited to be received. In the house shown opposite an ornamental pool lies in the centre of a garden surrounded by painted *trompe-l'oeil* pilasters.

"Just imagine: I was in Pompeii, perched on a narrow, ruined wall, when suddenly it shifted and then collapsed, throwing me straight down, head first, onto the antique marble floor beneath. I must confess, I can think of no better way to die, nor of any better place to be buried."

F. Mazois
Letter to Mlle Duval

When Garibaldi entered Naples in 1861, overturning the Bourbons, he offered the directorship of the museum and excavations to the French novelist Alexandre Dumas, author of *The Three Musketeers*. But Dumas was only prepared to make a short-term commitment to the post.

As Italy is united under Victor-Emmanuel II and Cavour, Pompeii's fortunes begin to change

The new king of Italy was aware of the prestige that his dynasty would gain from well-organized

Overall view of the excavations during the 19th century. In the foreground is the theatre quarter, with the gladiators' barracks; in the centre, a triumphal arch marks the position of the Temple of the Capitoline Triad and, therefore, the open square of the forum.

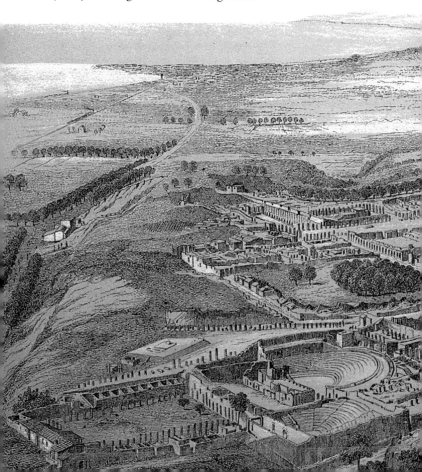

excavations at Pompeii. On 20 December 1860 he
put Giuseppe Fiorelli in charge of the excavations.
Fiorelli was a young numismatist already known for
his critical good sense and scientific integrity. He
soon established a scientific approach to archaeology,
keeping a written record of the excavations and
preparing a methodical plan for
uncovering the site quarter by
quarter and house by house,
with the aid of over
five hundred

Just to the right of
centre in this print
the S-curve of the Via
Consolare contrasts with
the regular grid-like
layout of roads in the
area just to the east of it.

In 1863 the excavations at Pompeii were the scene of intense activity. Hordes of workmen carry away the rubble in wicker baskets (left), while in the areas where buildings are being restored (right), builders are busy reconstructing roofs, re-righting columns and relaying lintels.

Around this time Fiorelli invented a way of casting the bodies that had been buried in ash. Liquid plaster was poured through a small hole, until the entire cavity had been filled. It was thus discovered that the volcanic ash had, in solidifying around the bodies of both humans and animals, moulded itself to their forms, defining every tiny fold of their clothes.

Overleaf: the restoration of the forum of Pompeii (cross-section). Detail of the Basilica of Apollo.

workmen. He divided Pompeii into regions and blocks, or *insulae,* allotting each house an identifying number; his system is still in use today.

To avoid the danger of houses collapsing into roads that had already been cleared, he excavated them from the roof downwards, gradually removing all debris from the site. In 1863 he invented a method of plaster casting that preserved the positions adopted by Pompeians in the

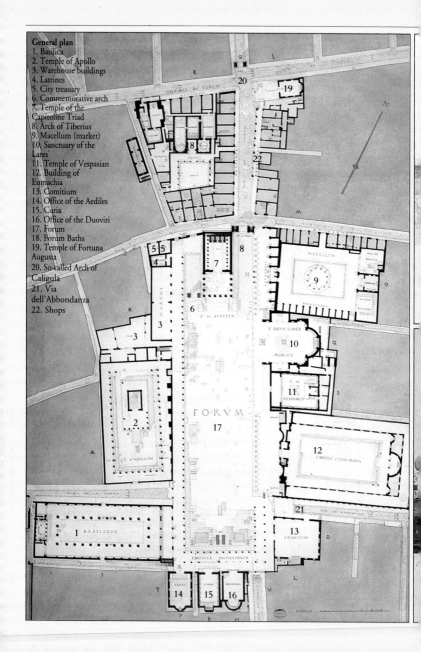

General plan
1. Basilica
2. Temple of Apollo
3. Warehouse buildings
4. Latrines
5. City treasury
6. Commemorative arch
7. Temple of the Capitoline Triad
8. Arch of Tiberius
9. Macellum (market)
10. Sanctuary of the Lares
11. Temple of Vespasian
12. Building of Eumachia
13. Comitium
14. Office of the Aediles
15. Curia
16. Office of the Duoviri
17. Forum
18. Forum Baths
19. Temple of Fortuna Augusta
20. So-called Arch of Caligula
21. Via dell'Abbondanza
22. Shops

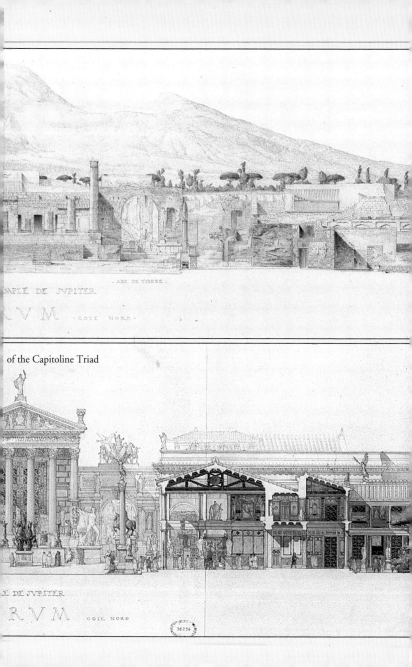

of the Capitoline Triad

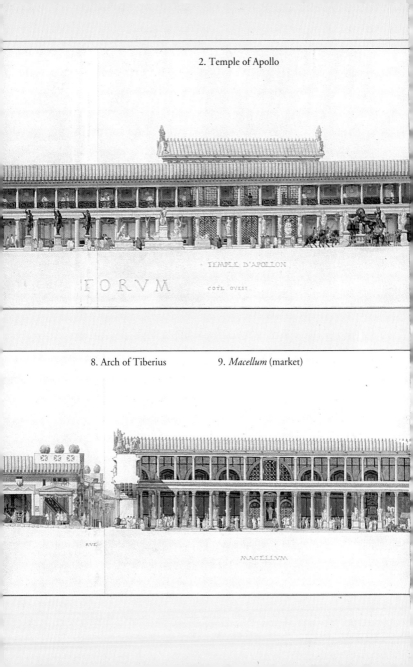

2. Temple of Apollo

TEMPLE D'APOLLON

CÔTÉ OUEST

FORVM

8. Arch of Tiberius 9. *Macellum* (market)

RVE

MACELLVM

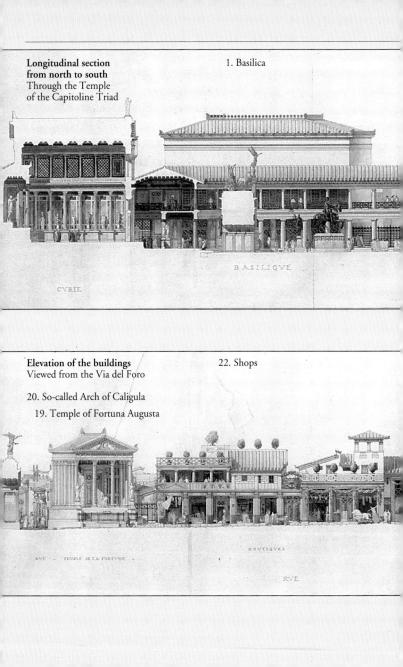

Longitudinal section from north to south
Through the Temple of the Capitoline Triad

1. Basilica

CVRIE

BASILIQVE

Elevation of the buildings
Viewed from the Via del Foro

22. Shops

20. So-called Arch of Caligula

19. Temple of Fortuna Augusta

RVE · TEMPLE DE LA FORTVNE ·

BOVTIQVES

RVE

The forum, which was brought to light from the early 19th century, was soon adopted in all the architectural academies of Europe as the very model of the classical square. This 1910 reconstruction was the fourth-year project of Léon Jaussely of Paris.

EDIFICE D'EVMACHIA. MARCHE · AUX · LAINES.

12. Building of Eumachia

21. Via dell'Abbondanza

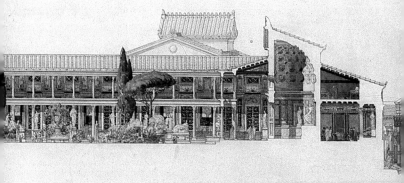

EDIFICE D'EVMACHIA

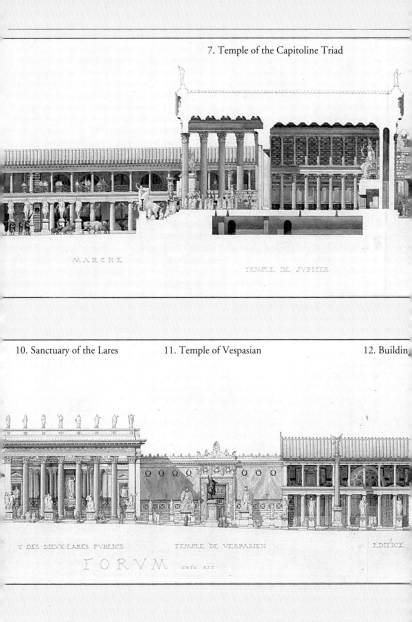

7. Temple of the Capitoline Triad

MARCHE

TEMPLE DE JUPITER

10. Sanctuary of the Lares   11. Temple of Vespasian   12. Buildin

T·DES·DIEVX·LARES·PVBLICS   TEMPLE DE VESPASIEN   EDIFICE

FORVM   COTE EST

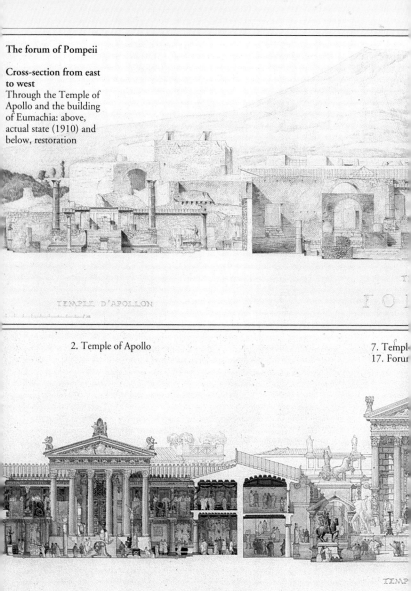

The forum of Pompeii

Cross-section from east to west
Through the Temple of Apollo and the building of Eumachia: above, actual state (1910) and below, restoration

TEMPLE D'APOLLON

2. Temple of Apollo

7. Templ
17. Forur

TEMPLE D'APOLLON

FO

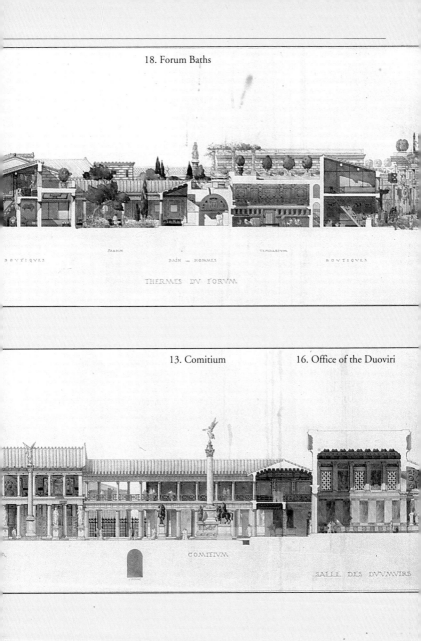

18. Forum Baths

BOVTIQVES   JARDIN   BAIN — HOMMES   TEPIDARIVM   BOVTIQVES

THERMES DV FORVM

13. Comitium   16. Office of the Duoviri

COMITIVM

SALLE DES DVVMVIRS

moment of death. The most intimate details of daily life in the city could at last be revealed. Using these techniques, Fiorelli identified the Lupanar, or brothel, a bakery and the House of Caecilius Jucundus (V, 1, 26). In 1875 he took on overall control of the museums, leaving his students to complete his work, which had emphasized the topographical cohesion of the excavations.

A Pompeian Golden Age: 1875-93

Michele Ruggiero, an architect who had formerly worked with Fiorelli, sought to extend the excavations eastwards, towards the Nolan Gate, by excavating the northernmost quarters of the city along the upper *decumanus*. In the process, the Central Baths were discovered. In Region IX the House of the Centenary (8, 3) – so named to commemorate the eighteenth centenary of the eruption – and *insulae* 4, 5, 6, 7 and 8 were excavated, followed by those in Region V on the Via di Nola and the Via Stabiana (1, 2, 3, 4). The excavation of *insula* 2 in Region VIII proved extremely difficult, as in this area the houses, which were several storeys high, were constructed on the slope of a hill formed by a prehistoric lava flow.

Another discovery of the 1880s were the cemeteries just outside the gates to the city; a few tombs were found near what is assumed to have been the road from Pompeii to Nocera (Nuceria), and two tombs were discovered at the Stabian Gate. Ruggiero was also responsible for the consolidation and restoration, *in situ*, of over six hundred paintings and of the atrium of the House of the Silver Wedding (V, 2) and the House of the Balcony (VII, 12, 28).

A new man in charge: the epigraphist Giulio de Petra

De Petra directed work on the site from 1893 to 1901, a period of painstaking work marked by the discovery of the House of the Vettii, now one of the most famous in Pompeii (VI, 15, 1), and the House of Lucretius Fronto (V, 4, 10). He continued to excavate the northern areas of the city and Regions V and VI. Towers X and XI of the outer wall were

The plan of a typical Pompeian house can be studied from that of the House of the Centenary, as it was reconstructed in 1903 by Jules-Léon Chifflot. It was made up of two basic elements: a native Italian-style house based around an atrium, and a Hellenistic house around a peristyle. A narrow corridor (*fauces*) led from the entrance to the atrium, where the roof sloped down on all sides towards an opening in the centre (*compluvium*). For a long while, it was in the main atrium – here, there is also a secondary atrium – that the household gathered for meals, work and rest. But it was an uncomfortable room, blackened by smoke (hence the name: from *ater*, black), and it was soon reduced to the role of providing a light-well and a source of fresh air. Opening off the atrium, opposite the entrance, was a large room (*tablinum*) flanked by two adjoining rooms (*alae*). Originally a dining room and bedroom, the *tablinum* came to be used simply as a reception room, giving access to the peristyle garden beyond, around which were arranged the bedrooms, the dining room (*triclinium*) and another reception room (*oecus*).

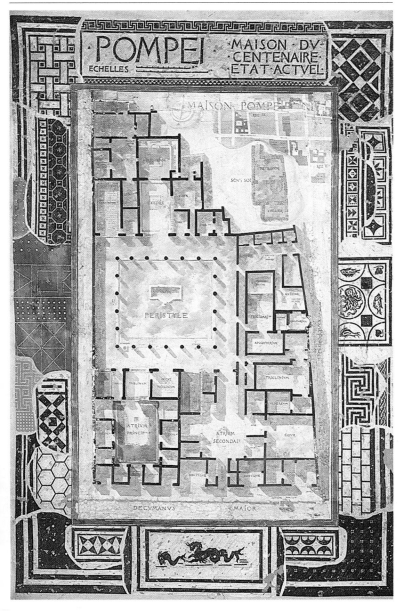

HELLE · 0.03 P·M'   POMPEI · MAISON · DV

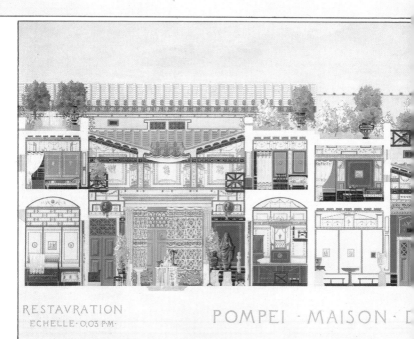

RESTAVRATION
ECHELLE · 0.03 · P·M·   POMPEI · MAISON · D

NAIRE · RESTAVRATION

NTENAIRE

Under the influence of the Hellenistic house, rooms gradually became specialized along more rational and aesthetically satisfying lines, as the 'service quarters' were moved further away from the fine reception rooms. An architectural innovation that had an impact throughout the city was the introduction of large windows into rooms looking out onto porticoes or the garden. Above: longitudinal section of the House of the Centenary; below: transverse section, between the two atriums.

found, and behind the basilica were discovered the remains of a temple dedicated to Venus Pompeiana, the tutelary goddess of the city. A superficial investigation was made of the Temple of Jupiter and the Temple of Apollo, but the main focus of attention shifted towards the surrounding countryside, the suburb called Pagus Augustus Felix Suburbanus, and private villas, like the Villa of the Mysteries. De Petra was above all responsible for the restoration of roofs, the covering of atria and peristyles, and the careful recreation of the inner gardens of certain houses – essential elements in restoring life and colour to the city.

Between 1901 and 1905 the historian Ettore País continued work on the northern quarters between Region V (*insulae* 3 and 4) and Region VI (*insulae* 15 and 16), thus completing the excavation of areas adjoining the Via Stabiana and Via di Nola. He also discovered what remained of the Vesuvian Gate and of the water tower that had once supplied the entire city.

As archaeologist succeeds archaeologist, the work becomes increasingly systematic

With the exception of a few tombs uncovered by the Vesuvian Gate and the Nolan Gate, no major finds mark the next directorship, that of Antonio Sogliano (1905-10). He devoted himself primarily to restoring the Corinthian *oecus* of the House of the Silver Wedding, the peristyle of the House of the Golden Cupids (VI, 17, 7), and the balcony of the Lupanar. His primary concern was for the conservation of Pompeii, and he perfected a wide range of technical measures for this purpose, many of which are still in use today.

Vittorio Spinazzola (1910-24) vigorously pursued a programme of work that was even more systematic than those that had preceded it. First, he proposed abandoning the excavation of the northern quarters of the city completely, in favour of the southern quarters. His aim was to link the city centre with the amphitheatre and to follow the Via dell'Abbondanza as far as the Sarnian Gate. This was an inspired plan, prompted by a concern with the realities of town

The House of Lucretius Fronto was excavated under Giulio de Petra in 1900. Methods had not progressed significantly since the previous century; workmen still carried the earth away in baskets, before emptying it into horse-drawn carts. They worked down through the surface layer of ash towards the interior of the house, restoring the structure as they went. As we can see here, the stucco surface of the columns was restored with considerable care.

planning, rather than the illusory satisfaction of making extraordinary discoveries; it sought to reveal the commercial life of the city through the external appearance of its main artery, rather than simply continuing to uncover more private houses.

But this plan had its drawbacks. By confining themselves to the frontages of the buildings on either side of the road – which, in the area being excavated, was 600 m long – the archaeologists not only lost the opportunity of excavating houses that were rich with promise, but were also forced to guess at the precise purpose of a shop, boutique, or building of unusual appearance, by interpreting the paintings, election posters and graffiti that covered their facades. In addition, they had to protect the facades from the weight of the damp earth that lay behind them.

Spinazzola therefore found it impossible to stick to his original plan, and when he came

upon buildings of particular interest, he decided to strike out into the *insula*, excavating as far as the alley behind. And so, for the first 400 m the excavations trace an irregular pattern, widening and contracting like the banks of a river; even today this uneven appearance remains.

Nevertheless, there were considerable advantages for the excavator in following a single street; it resulted in a unified restoration, the conservation of paintings and wall advertisements, and of shop furnishings. All this revealed a Pompeii that had been scarcely dreamed of, and which aroused the enthusiasm of all those who visited the site.

Working by this method, Spinazzola discovered the Fullonica Stephani (I, 6, 7), an industrial enterprise within a private house, and the *thermopolium*, or inn, of Asellina (IX, 11, 2). He chose to excavate the houses that appeared most wealthy: the House of Paquius Proculus (I, 7, 1), the House of the Cryptoporticus (I, 6, 2), the House of Lucius Ceius Secundus (I, 6, 15), the House of Trebius Valens (III, 2, 1) and that of Loreius Tiburtinus with its vast garden (II, 5, 2); he also

The Via dell' Abbondanza links the forum with the Sarnian Gate and, thus, with the amphitheatre. This photograph, taken in 1910, illustrates the criticisms that can be made of Spinazzola's methods. Although the work initially appeared impressive, the facades had to be shored up to prevent them from collapsing.

uncovered the House of the Moralist (V, 1, 18). But his name remains most closely associated with the excavation of the Via dell'Abbondanza.

Under the 'regime' of Amedeo Maiuri (1924-61), the excavations at Pompeii took a new direction and acquired an added dimension. Maiuri must above all be credited with perfecting our knowledge of the history of the city through more extensive and more carefully conducted excavations. It is with him that we enter the age of scientific archaeology which alone can preserve the miracle of Pompeii. His successors A. de Franciscis, F. Zevi and Mrs Irulli Cerulli have followed the same path.

A medeo Maiuri casts an excited eye over the Venus of the Shell, a magnificent mural found in the House of Julia Felix. It was uncovered for the second time in 1952-3.

The Pompeian miracle

An average city inhabited by average people, Pompeii would have achieved a comfortable mediocrity and passed peacefully into the silence of history, had the sudden catastrophe of the volcanic eruption not suddenly wiped it from the world of the living.

Frozen for centuries, myriad messages about the daily life of the Pompeian people are still there for us to read, if we can decipher them. In Pompeii the ancient world speaks to us directly, touches us through the thousands of events of an apparently normal, everyday world. The workmen are busy mixing plaster to cover the cryptoporticus of the Villa of the Mysteries; the altar tables are prepared for the priests of Isis....

Pompeii is so moving and fascinating because we rediscover there the occupations, feelings, dreams and fantasies of men and women who seem so close to us, so full of life. The real miracle of Pompeii lies in the fact that, so many centuries after its disastrous fate, it can vividly conjure up the joys and sorrows, hopes and fears of a small provincial town which entered the annals of history in spite of itself. Pompeii is not the privileged domain of specialists; it belongs to the whole of humanity.

The city revealed to us by the excavations has a long history. How did it develop from a small community of fishermen and farmers in the 10th century BC into the flourishing city of twenty thousand inhabitants that was buried beneath the ash on 24 August AD 79?

CHAPTER 2
LIFE IN POMPEII

Before the eruption of AD 79, on 5 February AD 62, a violent earthquake destroyed a triumphal arch and the Temple of the Capitoline Triad, with its colonnaded portico.

The varied saga of occupying forces: Oscans, Greeks, Etruscans, Samnites, Romans

The original village, inhabited by the Oscans, a native Italian people, was built on a steep volcanic ridge produced by a prehistoric lava flow. It probably lay at the heart of Regions VII and VIII (see pp. 46-7), where the irregular pattern of the roads, which survived all later occupations, clearly illustrates the primitive nature of the settlement.

In the 6th century BC the Greeks settled here, taking advantage of the site's excellent strategic position on an important maritime trade route. They built a Doric temple on a spur of land overlooking the valley of the river Sarno and the sea, and introduced the cult of Apollo. For the Greeks, however, Pompeii was only an outpost, allowing them to maintain control of the port and sea outlets from the hinterland, rather than a permanent settlement.

At some point between 524 and 474 BC, the Etruscans occupied the town, though they have left no trace of any specific building work. From 474 to 424 BC, Pompeii again experienced strong Greek influence; temples were restored, the town was fortified by a surrounding wall, and enlarged with the construction of Region VI. This followed the principles of the architect of the Piraeus, Hippodamus of Miletus, in that it was laid out according to a regular geometric grid, with numerous roads providing access and communication.

The Osco-Greek town was next brutally conquered by the Samnites, rough mountaindwellers from the Abruzzi and Calabria, who in 424 BC swept down on the Greek 'colonies' on the coast. The Samnites who settled on the coastal plains became known as *Campani*, and so Pompeii became a Campanian town; the people adopted the Oscan tongue once more, as it was common to both the original occupants of the town and the new arrivals.

The Oscan alphabet (below left) included some signs that stood for letters, and others that stood for syllables. The Oscan language was spoken by all Pompeians until the creation of the Roman colony and continued in use amongst the general population for a good while afterwards.

Pompeii retained certain traces of the Greek period of occupation. The cult of Apollo, for example, celebrated during the Archaic period (7th century BC) under the influence of the maritime empire of Cumae, survived the Etruscan occupation (524-474 BC). It was adopted by the Oscans and Campanians, and later, of course, by the Romans. The Temple of Apollo was built on rising ground, dominating the main routes through the city. It is seen here as reconstructed by the Romans. On the left is the podium of the temple itself, where the cult statue stood, and on the right is a colonnaded courtyard, made of tufa and stucco. On a level with the fifth column stands a Herm surmounted by a marble bust of Mercury.

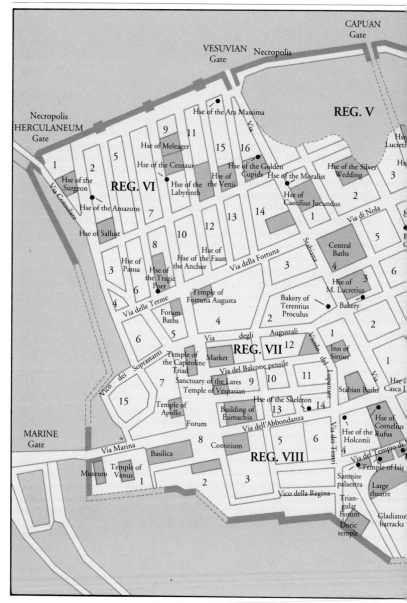

CAPUAN Gate

VESUVIAN Gate   Necropolis

Necropolis
HERCULANEUM Gate

REG. V

Hse of the Ara Massima

Hse of Meleager

Hse of the Centaur

Hse of the Surgeon

Hse of the Labyrinth

Hse of the Amazons

Hse of Sallust

REG. VI

Hse of the Golden Cupids

Hse of the Vettii

Hse of the Moralist

Hse of the Silver Wedding

Hse of Caecilius Jucundus

Via di Nola

Central Baths

Hse of M. Lucretius

Bakery of Terentius Proculus   Bakery

Hse of Pansa

Hse of the Tragic Poet

Hse of the Faun

Hse of the Anchor

Via delle Terme

Via della Fortuna

Temple of Fortuna Augusta

Forum Baths

Via degli   Augustali

Temple of the Capitoline Triad

Market

Via del Balcone pensile

REG. VII

Inn of Sittius

Sanctuary of the Lares

Temple of Vespasian

Stabian Baths

Hse of Casca L

Temple of Apollo

Building of Eumachia

Hse of the Skeleton

Via dell'Abbondanza

Hse of Cornelius Rufus

Hse of the Holconii

MARINE Gate

Via Marina

Basilica

Comitium

REG. VIII

Via del Tempio di

Temple of Venus

Museum

Vico della Regina

Samnite palaestra

Temple of Isis

Large theatre

Triangular Forum

Doric temple

Gladiator barracks

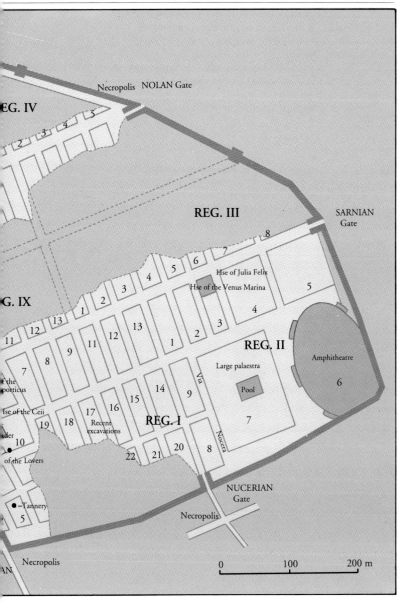

REG. IV

Necropolis   NOLAN Gate

5

2   3   4

REG. III

SARNIAN
Gate

8

7

5   6

4   5   Hse of Julia Felix

G. IX   3   Hse of the Venus Marina   5

1   2   3   4

13   13   3   2   1

11   12   12   1   2   REG. II

11   9   11   12   Amphitheatre

7   8   Large palaestra   6

the
porticus   9   14   Pool

Ise of the Ceii   17   16   15   9

der   19   18   Recent   REG. I   7

10   excavations   Via Nocera

of the Lovers   22   21   20   8

●–Tannery

5   NUCERIAN
Gate

Necropolis

Necropolis

AN   0   100   200 m

Although the Romans subjected the Samnites who had remained in their mountainous homeland to fierce military attack, they formed an alliance with the Campani. Neither Pyrrhus, king of Epirus, in *c.* 280 BC, nor Hannibal in 216 BC – to whom all the other cities of Campania swore allegiance – could shake Pompeii's loyalty to Rome.

As a defence against its turbulent neighbours and a

guarantee of independence from Rome, Pompeii remained throughout this period a fortified city. Between 424 and 89 BC it was surrounded with an increasingly solid system of fortifications: two parallel walls of black tufa and limestone, buttressed by an *agger*, or earth mound, with twelve square towers straddling the ramparts. From north to south these fortifications were built over the old city walls, showing that the town had not expanded in that direction, though it had developed considerably in the whole of the eastern sector. The 3014 m of urban perimeter that we see today were therefore established

Between the Herculaneum Gate and the Vesuvian Gate – shown here, in the background – three towers, including this one, Tower X, punctuate the Samnite fortifications.

by the Samnites. This impressive defensive wall defined the city's limits, beyond which lay the burial grounds.

The Samnites also established the main arteries of the city; their aim was to link the Triangular Forum and its complex of monuments with the civil forum by the present-day Via del Tempio di Iside and the Via dei Teatri, while the Via Stabiana (or Via Pompeiana, as it is called in an inscription) crossed the city from north to south, continuing by a bridge over the river Sarno as far as the town of Stabiae.

In March 90 BC the Samnite towns rose up against Rome, and this time Pompeii joined the rebels. The war against the 'allies' under the leadership of Sulla proved difficult and prolonged. Pompeii was besieged, and its walls were bombarded with huge stone balls marked with the name of Sulla; the tufa still bears their indelible imprint. Between summer 90 and autumn 89 BC, the city succumbed. Thereafter Pompeii was Roman but at peace, a situation that was to last until that fateful day in AD 79.

Monumental districts, residential districts

Rome brought no great changes, as far as town planning was concerned; the Roman way of life was introduced into districts that owed their essentially monumental or residential character to the Samnite era, even after they had undergone reconstruction or restoration (especially after the earthquake of AD 62).

It was in the forum, which was at once the religious, political and commercial centre, that the heart of the Roman colony lay. The Temple of the Capitoline Triad (or Temple of Jupiter), the Temple of the Lares and the Temple of Vespasian were all to be found here. Political matters were dealt with in the Curia and in the offices of the magistrates, while the

The road bed was made up of tightly packed chalk or trachyte blocks. The way it was designed helped pedestrians to get around the city. When it rained, they could keep their feet dry by crossing the street on large stepping stones, which had space left between them for the passage of cartwheels (top).

market (*macellum*), the building of Eumachia, the wool and cloth market, and the *mensa ponderaria*, or office of weights and measures, represented the commercial centre of the city.

The old Triangular Forum now became part of the theatre quarter,

The Vico di Mercurio (left) leads from Tower XI to the forum. The so-called Arch of Caligula is in the background. In the foreground are the Houses of Meleager and of the Centaur.

acting as a foyer to the large theatre and offering an area to stroll in during the interval. Also nearby were the Samnite *palaestra*, or sports ground, the Temple of Isis and the Temple of Jupiter Meilichios, so this part of the town combined both religious and athletic functions. The area around the amphitheatre, to the south-east, included a second, larger *palaestra*. This was the most spacious quarter of the city, where crowds of spectators could enjoy the shade of the plane trees, sampling the many delicacies that were on sale there.

In the south-west corner of the forum lies the basilica, with its three vast aisles. Justice was dispensed from the tribunal that stands at the end of the central nave (above). The raised platform of the tribunal is ornamented with six Corinthian pillars, topped by a smaller colonnade with a decorative pediment.

The Pompeian house: architectural mastery

The architect François Mazois (see p. 25) executed fine reconstruction drawings showing every detail of the roof and *compluvium* of a typical atrium (opposite, above: view from above and elevation). The *impluvium* at floor level would have corresponded with the open square above formed by the four slopes of the roof. The system of roof trusses, beams and rafters is clearly illustrated (opposite, below), together with the arrangement of flat edging tiles (*tegulae*) and rounded tiles, which concealed the joins (*imbrices*). In summer the Pompeians dined in the open air, just as they do today, taking their couches (*triclinia*) out under the peristyle or into the garden. To avoid having to carry around such heavy pieces of furniture, carved stone *triclinia* were often placed in the garden around a stone table. Close by, a small shrine was provided for libations. The section and schematic view (left) show a particularly simple *triclinium*, with no pergola to offer shade or fountain to cool the air.

Decorative schemes: painting set free

The wealthy citizen of Pompeii used paintings to create a *musée imaginaire* within his own home; these decorative schemes therefore help us to penetrate his spiritual life and to assess his tastes. There is no longer any secret about how Pompeian paintings were executed; pigments were mixed in a solution of lime and soap, with a little added wax, then the finished painting was burnished (using a metal trowel, a marble or glass cylinder, or special polishing stone), and buffed up with a clean cloth. In one of the dining rooms of the House of the Vettii (opposite) panels depict mythological subjects. The elaborate architectural vistas are typical of the fourth style of wall-painting in Pompeii. In the third style (above left) the architectural elements are merely ornamental, creating the impression of a closed recess; the landscape looks more like a painting than a realistic view through a window into space. The still life below left celebrates a taste for beautifully crafted objects, displaying a collection of silver worthy of the House of Menander.

Pompeian gardens: the taming of nature

The increasing amount of space devoted to gardens corresponds to the Romans' love of nature. A garden provided greenery and coolness, but was also charged with dreams; some Pompeians sought to emulate the palace gardens of the great Hellenistic princes. Flowering plants, plane and cypress trees, ivy, bay and oleander were combined to create effects worthy of a large park, while the careful arrangement of clumps of trees and flower borders underlined their desire to introduce an architectural structure into their gardens. Through paintings, this taste for greenery and for formality was continued into the house itself. In both the frieze above and the mural below, wooden balustrades made of interwoven laths define semicircular and rectangular alcoves, which create the illusion of a series of planes receding into depth. By means of these alcoves, the painter introduces into the garden, at regular intervals, fountains, ceramic vases and birds, which perch on the wooden pergola or strut about on the lawn.

Virtually all the remaining districts of the city were residential, and their development during the Roman period is punctuated by the construction of the public baths that were such an essential part of daily life in Pompeii. The oldest of these, the Stabian Baths, had been built in the Samnite period; but the Forum Baths date from the establishment of the Roman colony, and the Central Baths were still under construction at the time of the eruption. They all stand on main roads, at the edge of the old Oscan centre, where the winding streets in the shadow of the Lupanar were the haunt of prostitutes.

Certain streets, where *thermopolia* and taverns were interspersed with shops, had a more commercial flavour. And, surprisingly, in the heart of the city there remained a semi-rustic quarter (in Region I), where several summer *triclinia* (outdoor couches) lay amid rural gardens; there was even a vineyard where wine could be purchased. As an active, commercial city, Pompeii retained a rustic character that was much appreciated by lovers of good food and fine wines.

When he created the colony in 80 BC, Sulla made Pompeii a mini-Rome responsible for its own internal affairs

Supreme authority rested with the two *duoviri*, who made legal pronouncements and were responsible for administering public funds and presiding over meetings of the town council. Below them, two further magistrates, or *aediles*, were in charge of less important administrative tasks, such as road maintenance, the supervision of the markets and organization of the police. Each of these officials had a building on the forum for his offices and records. The Curia, also on the forum, was the seat of the municipal council, which was made up of one hundred *decuriones*, most of whom were former magistrates.

'Fuscus and Vaccula advise you to vote for A. Vettius Firmus, candidate for the aedileship'

In July of each year Pompeians voted for the municipal magistrates. As early as the spring, election

The vast houses belonging to important Pompeians always contained the essential garden, like this one in the House of the Faun, where clumps of bushes blend with the ornamental pools and niches for sacred statues.

Groups of neighbours would have their names inscribed on the house of an electoral candidate in red letters. Here they express their support for Lucretius Fronto and Caius Julius Polybius, whom they judge worthy of the *res publica*, the civic community, and of the office of *duovir*, or magistrate.

fever hit the city. Walls were covered in posters painted in red or black. As there were no hoardings reserved specifically for posters, a citizen would express his personal support for a particular candidate by devoting part of the front of his house to him. The inhabitants of a quarter (*vicini*) would often

employ advertising companies to whitewash the walls, frequently working right through the night to erase the inscriptions of the previous year.

In contrast to present-day political practice, it was not considered appropriate for the candidate himself to call for votes; others sought them on his behalf by presenting him as the man most worthy of the office. There were no elaborate professions of faith, no boasts about a brilliant career, no promises to support a public building programme, implement tax cuts or improve the quality of the roads; all that mattered was the testimony of others to the candidate's good moral character.

At the time of the Pompeian catastrophe, the Jewish communities started the rumour that the eruption of Vesuvius was divine vengeance for Titus' destruction of the Temple of Jerusalem eight years earlier.

This explains why one important citizen standing for election, C. Julius Polybius, enraged by the fact that Cuculla and Zmyrina, two prostitutes at his local bar, had declared their support for him, demanded that their inscriptions be erased; clearly, to be sponsored by people of such ill repute could do his cause no good at all.

Although women could neither stand for election nor vote, they nevertheless played an active role in the election campaigns, which shed fascinating light on relationships between neighbours, on ties of interdependence, and on the influence of corporate and religious bodies on the political process.

Though Pompeii was self-governing in municipal matters, it was still subject to imperial decree

Once elected, the magistrates would never venture to involve themselves in broader political issues or to question the objectives defined in Rome by the emperor and his ministers. Their horizon was limited to the administration of municipal affairs, the most urgent concern after the earthquake of AD 62 being the reconstruction of the city. With the arrival of each new emperor, the city displayed its loyalty; the imperial cult was celebrated annually by a *flamen*, or special priest, and there were increasing numbers of shrines to the Augustan Virtues.

In general, Rome interfered little in the internal affairs of Pompeii, except when public order was threatened. In AD 59, for example, when a brawl erupted in the amphitheatre between people from Pompeii and Nocera (see pp. 108-9), the *duoviri* then in office, the brothers Grosphi, were dismissed; two replacements were selected, and Nero appointed a law-giving prefect (*iure dicundo*) to supervise them. The emperor also suspended the games, only to reinstate them a little later to universal joy, thereby underlining his omnipotence and reinforcing his popularity.

Another imperial intervention occurred when Vespasian dispatched T. Suedius Clemens to restore order to the tax registers and to reclaim city land that had been appropriated by corrupt entrepreneurs. At no point did the Pompeians consider this an unacceptable attack on their autonomy; on the contrary, through this 'most holy' judge, they rendered homage to his noble master.

Constructed during the closing years of the 1st century BC by Marcus Tullius, the Temple of Fortuna Augusta, which stands to the north of the forum on the Via del Foro, imitated the structure of the Temple of the Capitoline Triad, with two flights of steps – one on either side of the central altar – leading to a platform at the foot of the podium. Eight columns with Corinthian capitals, four of them forming the facade, support the portico in front of the *cella*. The statue of Fortuna Augusta, which stood on a pedestal at the back of the sanctuary, reminded the worshippers that the emperor brought them good luck, and thus ensured the happiness of every Pompeian citizen.

How did the people of Pompeii earn a living? Was the town full of individuals who, attracted by the mild climate and beautiful countryside of Campania, had retired to Pompeii with their lifetime's savings? Or did they work hard, struggling, after the earthquake of AD 62, to confront the misfortune that had struck both rich and poor alike?

CHAPTER 3

EARNING A LIVING

By now bread was no longer made at home; Pompeians bought it each day from the bakery, a sign of the development of small-scale trade. Mercury, god of commerce, appears everywhere.

Lucrum gaudium, 'profit is joy': so runs the motto inscribed around the edge of the *impluvium* in a modest house belonging to a wood-turner. Elsewhere, in the entrance hall of a more wealthy dwelling owned by the two important citizens Siricus and Numerianus, a mosaic inscription again pays tribute to profit: *salve lucru*. Mercury, the god of commerce, is omnipresent, whether on the sales counter of an inn or on the wall of a fulling mill.

The propertied classes: profit from the land

Campania has always been an agricultural paradise. The fertile slopes of Vesuvius were dotted with estates where, between rows of vines and olive trees, cereals, vegetables and animal fodder were grown. The cultivation of spelt, a variety of durum wheat, enabled farmers to obtain two harvests a year, which helped to enrich the owners of wine-producing properties like the Villa of the Mysteries; here, a wine press and cellars, where round-bellied earthenware jars (*dolia*) held the harvests of wine and oil, point to production of a very high quality. The rearing of animals also flourished. Eumachia, the rich owner of the building on the forum, married a certain Numistrius, the owner of pastures and flocks of sheep. In a pen at his villa pigs and sheep were guarded by dogs.

The city itself required what was virtually an extensive market-garden suburb to keep it supplied with food; the gardens of Pompeii (*horti pompeiani*) are still famous today for their onions and herbs, as well as for their honey, which was used to sweeten the wine.

Money earned through the land, concentrated in the hands of a few important individuals, brought them political influence as well as economic power. Most of the members of the decurion council were freeborn wealthy landowners.

Bread and garum: the two major food industries

Basic foodstuffs were mainly produced by small tradesmen and, occasionally, by the wealthy owners of the agricultural estates. Bakeries can be identified

This blue amphora still contained wine when it was discovered in a tomb. It is decorated with pastoral and Bacchic scenes, divided by elegantly curling vine tendrils. For the people of Pompeii, wine was also the drink of immortality.

This round loaf, found in an oven, was divided into eight portions – a tradition carried on in Campania down to the present day.

from their millstones of grey-black tufa, which were turned by slaves with the aid of a wooden handle (*mola trusatilis*), or by a horse or donkey led by a slave (*mola asinaria*). The baker kneaded the dough, then baked the bread in an elaborate oven, before selling it in the adjoining shop; pâtissiers operated from smaller premises where they stored their many cake moulds.

Garum, which Seneca hated on account of its foul smell, was a sauce which must have resembled the

Lava millstones are set up ready for use in the courtyard of this bread factory. In the foreground stands the rotating, funnel-shaped *catillus*, which held the grain. In the background is the oven.

Vietnamese *nuoc-mam*, made of dried fish with salt added as a preservative. Its production was generally the monopoly of prosperous families, such as the Umbricii, because of the amount of initial investment required. A. Umbricius Scaurus, *duovir* under Claudius, supplied *garum* wholesale to a variety of retail outlets. The quality depended on the type of fish used: tuna, mackerel and moray eel for the more delicate varieties, and anchovies for *garum* intended for poor men and slaves.

Spinners, fullers and dyers

Sheep-breeding supplied a flourishing woollen industry, controlled once again by the top families, which employed a whole army of craftsmen. The fine building of Eumachia on the forum, where raw wool and finished cloth were probably sold, symbolizes the importance of the industry.

Once it had been washed, degreased and carded, the wool was sent to the spinners. The woollen

threads were then stretched over a vertical or horizontal loom, ready for weaving. Spinning and weaving were often carried out by the female slaves of a household, the cloth being sent to be treated by the fullers and dyers. The fulling process was carried out by the *coactiliarii*, who trod the finished cloth in a mixture of fuller's earth, potash, soda and urine. Once it had been rinsed and dried, brushed and bleached with sulphur or dyed in bright colours, such as purple or saffron yellow, it was ready to go on sale. Other workshops had the job of putting new life into old cloth by changing its colour. M. Vecilius Verecundus, one of the great fulling-mill owners, was an eminent member of the industrial bourgeoisie in Pompeii.

At the dyeing workshop of M. Vecilius Verecundus (above left) the workers first plunge the cloth into vats of dye, then hold it up to judge the quality of the result.

The concentration of wealth

After the earthquake of AD 62 the most urgent task was to reconstruct the city, and in order to produce sufficient quantities of tiles and bricks, the profitable export of wine and *garum* was stepped up. Increasing numbers of amphorae had to be manufactured for the export of these products, and as the wine- and *garum*-producers also tended to own the kilns, as well as the brick and tile factories essential for rebuilding, wealth became increasingly concentrated in the hands of a fortunate few.

Trade was booming: Pompeian landowners exported their agricultural surpluses, while products

To raise the tangled nap of the cloth, the workman on the left brushes it with an instrument to which are fixed thistles, thorns and prickles. The bell-shaped wicker frame on the right is designed to support the lengths of fabric while they are drying or being bleached with sulphur. The second workman carries a hot dish containing the burning sulphur.

arrived from overseas via the *Sarnus pompeianus*, or river Sarno. Thanks to its port, Pompeii was classified as an emporium, or entrepôt. Pictures of ships, graffiti and mosaic emblems such as anchors often indicate the homes of shipowners. Pompeian wine was exported to Gaul from as early as the 1st century BC, and Pompeian tiles have been found as far away as Dalmatia. Pompeian traders, who constituted a veritable diaspora throughout the Mediterranean, wove a complex network of contacts with the Orient, Egypt, Africa, and even Asia, their caravans reaching as far afield as the ports of Syria and Palestine, and, via the Red Sea and the canal of Nechao II, Alexandria.

The merchant bankers of Pompeii

To get an idea of the range of these Pompeian fortunes we can study the accounts that have been discovered in certain houses. For example, on 3 and 5 July 1875 more than 150 writing tablets were unearthed in the house of the merchant banker L. Caecilius Jucundus, on the eastern side of the Via Stabiana. They had originally been covered with a thin film of wax – hence their name, *tabulae ceratae* – and, as they still bore the marks made with the point of a stylus, it was possible to read what had been written on them. They were receipts (*apochae*) for the years AD 52 to 62, drawn up by Jucundus himself, by his secretary, or occasionally by the person who had just received the loan. Jucundus acted as a broker, lending capital to merchants in return for a fee. The amounts involved vary between 342 and 38,079 sesterces, an average of 8502 sesterces per transaction, which indicates quite considerable fortunes. Although he was a tax-farmer for the colony's four taxes, the banker was only among the fairly well-off

This bronze portrait bust of Lucius Caecilius Jucundus, the most famous banker in Pompeii, was found in the atrium of his house. He has the face of a realist, with a hint of provincial roughness, the ironic expression of his eyes reflecting the businessman's astute intelligence.

families of the city, and was not a member of the true oligarchy.

The wealth of Pompeians can also be assessed from the treasures they snatched up as they fled from the rain of ash

These amounts of money, which must correspond to what the average citizen happened to have readily available in cash, range from about 3000 to 10,000 sesterces. Twenty-six of them represent large sums of money: the highest was 9448 sesterces; six of the finds were over 4000; and the remainder were between 1000 and 4000 sesterces. These were plainly wealthy citizens.

In about sixty other cases the average amount was approximately 200 sesterces. Whether they involve significant sums or small change – the poor had on them only a few copper coins ('asses') to cover the cost of food – these finds clearly indicate the scale of incomes in Pompeii.

The workers: labourers, employees and shopkeepers

First, there were those whose only capital was their hands. Slaves or freedmen, they carried out work in the fields, tending the vines, picking grapes, ploughing, harvesting and hay-making, caring for the orchards and growing vegetables.

Other workers were employed in the bakeries, and around the vats of *garum* or the fulling tanks, amid

For keeping his accounts, the banker used a rigid wooden tablet covered with a thin film of wax, and a folding tablet, prepared in the same way, in which he recorded each business transaction. The circular box, or *capsa*, was used to store rolls of papyrus.

Pieces of gold and silver were discovered in this silver purse, carried by a chain, which was found in the wealthy House of Menander.

These putti, or cupids, in the House of the Vettii symbolize the various activities of the Pompeian guilds. On the far left, the pharmacist cupid is shaking a prepared medicine in a glass retort. Dangerous products are stored in the medicine cabinet behind him. Above left, the silversmith cupid is busy fashioning a piece of jewelry; a pair of Roman scales and a smaller assay balance indicate the precision with which precious metals had to be weighed. A blacksmith cupid introduces his tongs into the fierce flames of the forge, below left, while blowing through some form of pipe to heat up the embers. On the right, another cupid is putting the finishing touches to a large round dish made of gold.

the sickening smells of the tanneries. A vast industrial workforce manufactured a whole variety of bronze and silver objects, from safes to mirrors and brazier stands, from high-precision metalwork for architectural, surveying and surgical instruments, to jewelry that would satisfy even the most demanding customer.

At the market on the forum, along the pavements and in the shade of the plane trees in the square near the amphitheatre, there swarmed crowds of smalltraders, shoe- and fabric-sellers, pedlars of pottery, mule-drivers and porters. Advertisers, doctors and painters could also be found there, alongside musicians and school-teachers. Together they constituted what today would be called the service industries.

And what of the unemployed? Only rarely were people truly unemployed; there was always some work to be found – seasonal work, at least, with all the hay-making, harvesting and grape-picking that went on in the large estates around the city. And, of course, every time a ship came into the Pompeian port on the river Sarnus manpower was required to unload its cargo. Above all, after the earthquake of AD 62, the task of reconstructing the city ensured plenty of work for everyone.

Every ancient Mediterranean city also had its share of beggars who survived on public charity; in Pompeii the blind and disabled did not starve to death. There was always a small coin, a crust of bread, or a bowl of stew to supply their basic needs.

The great variety of surgical instruments – needles, speculum, scalpel, forceps, scissors – illustrates the development of medical science during the 1st century AD. Like the brazier (left), they testify to the high quality and precision of Pompeian metalwork.

Right: A craftsman strikes the chisel with a mallet in order to make notches in a piece of wood. Carpenters played a vital role in the construction of all new buildings, either on an individual basis, or as members of organized professional bodies.

Charity eased the misery of the poorest in society and of the handicapped. Here, a lady of quality accompanied by a servant offers a coin to a blind man (left).

A market was held each week under the portico of the forum, which was decorated with garlands of flowers for the occasion (left). The stalls were set out at pavement level. On the right, a shoemaker shows off his wares to two seated female customers, while others wait their turn. On the left, an elderly man appears to have fallen asleep over the take-away cooked meals he is offering for sale; large jars contain the stews and sauces.

A city where social harmony reigned

In this population, estimated at 20,000 inhabitants (8000 slaves and 12,000 freedmen, of whom 4200 were adults), rich and poor lived happily side by side, just as the Greeks, Etruscans, Oscans and Latins had done down through the centuries.

The city experienced no inter-class strife or racial discrimination; slaves and freedmen shared in the fortunes of their masters, and relationships of economic interdependence enabled every man to earn his daily bread. And all the more easily, since basic foodstuffs were cheaper in Pompeii than in many other cities of the empire (see pp. 184-5).

Women of the classical world had achieved relative emancipation long before the 1st century AD. They no longer lived cloistered lives in the gynaeceum, subject to their husband's will. They mingled with the crowds in the forum, participating in all the hustle and bustle of street life. Many Pompeian women even declared themselves the equal of men.

CHAPTER 4
THE ROLE OF
WOMEN

In the privacy of her own home, a woman supervises her child's reading, while the servant busies herself with preparing a meal.

The colonnade around the forum, where salesmen have set up their stalls on the pavement, is festooned with brightly coloured garlands. A shoemaker sings the praises of his wares to two women customers seated in front of him on a bench. A wealthy lady, accompanied by her slave, has just given alms to a blind beggar dressed in rags. The frescoes in the House of Julia Felix (pp. 74-5) show clearly that women were present in the streets as well as in the houses of Pompeii.

Once upon a time... there was a future empress

The life of Sabina Poppaea begins like a fairytale. She was born into a rich Pompeian family who owned two sumptuously appointed houses: the House of the Golden Cupids, whose peristyle is decorated with several theatrical masks, and the House of Menander, where 118 pieces of silverware were discovered. Sabina was beautiful, and well aware of it. Her fellow citizens made no secret of their admiration for her; one wall bears the words: 'May you blossom forever, Sabina, preserve your beauty and your maidenhood for many years'.

But she paid no heed to this advice, sacrificing her virtue to the Emperor Nero, who married her in AD 62. This was the very year in which an earthquake destroyed her home town, and Sabina must surely have prevailed upon her husband to help the townspeople, just as she later asked him to authorize the people of Pompeii to hold gladiatorial contests; Nero had imposed a ban on the games in AD 59 to punish the Pompeians for having massacred their neighbours

The wealthy and charming Sabina Poppaea, who had property in Pompeii itself, also owned a sumptuously decorated country villa (right), recently discovered at Oplontis (Torre Annunziata).

This gold *bulla*, or amulet (above left) and a bracelet in the shape of a snake may have been part of her personal collection of jewelry.

from Nocera in the arena. Permission was granted, and the Pompeians were overjoyed. They expressed their excitement by writing on the walls of their city graffiti that were found centuries later: 'Three cheers for imperial decrees; three cheers for the decisions of the emperor and empress. Long live the Empress Poppaea.' A few years later they remembered the emperor's gesture and held games to celebrate Nero's fortunate escape from the Naples earthquake of AD 64.

Not even a rich landowner like Julia Felix could escape the effects of an earthquake

The House of Julia Felix occupied a whole *insula*, or block. Vast, beautiful and magnificently decorated, this residence bears witness to the wealth and good taste of its owner. As in all Pompeian houses, the rooms were arranged around an interior garden where fountains murmured and decorative plants complemented the architecture. The peristyle was made up of slim fluted marble pilasters, crowned by Corinthian capitals. It framed the entrance to the dining room, the finest room in the house, which was richly furnished with marble couches for the guests. The end wall was covered with stones to create the

These paintings in the House of Julia Felix are not mere exercises in illusionism, but rather proclaim a taste for elegant objects, for succulent fruits that evoke the glorious riches of Pompeian agriculture. On the shelf stand a bronze mortar with a long-handled spoon, a plate of large eggs and a pewter *oenochoe*, or wine jug; four thrushes and a fringed cloth are hanging on the wall. A small amphora containing some precious old wine leans against the shelf.

effect of a nymph's grotto, and water trickled softly onto the marble steps of a fountain, creating a wonderful freshness. Yet Julia Felix was not satisfied with such dazzling luxury; in her garden she preferred to relax in a summer *triclinium* that was more rustic in character, the carved beds and table painted in bright colours. Every room in the house was painted with scenes taken from life, which evoked the noise and bustle of the forum, or with still-lifes, in which the artists created an illusion of depth from arrangements of ordinary domestic objects, skilfully using light to throw the riches of nature into high relief.

This crystal bowl overflows with fruit; apples, pears, apricots, pomegranates and a bunch of well-ripened, dark purple grapes display their full and luscious forms. An apple has fallen from the bowl; a pomegranate has split open. Further down, a pot filled with grapes and an amphora await the pleasure of the guests.

We can perhaps imagine the real Julia Felix through the features of this noble Campanian lady, with her rounded face and plump neck, set off by her straight, dark hair parted in the centre. Her expression is thoughtful, almost melancholy.

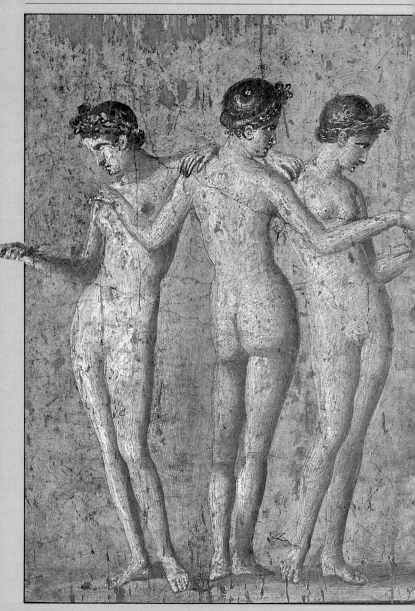

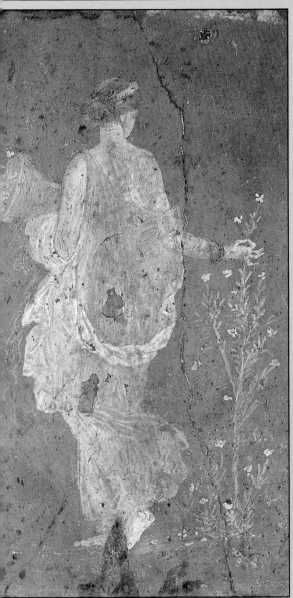

An age of beauty

The gods and goddesses of the classical world were very closely associated with ordinary mortals, and so in paintings it is often hard to distinguish a mythological subject from a scene of everyday life. The bodies of the three Graces (far left) express youthful awkwardness rather than sensuality, suggesting a trio of young girls surprised without their clothes rather than three striking and voluptuous goddesses. They bring a discreet charm and a hint of innocent eroticism to this pictorial commonplace. Similarly, is it the goddess Flora picking flowers to make up a 'divine' bouquet, or simply the lady of the house, the *domina*, wishing to decorate one of her rooms (left), as she walks through the garden, gracefully draped in a coloured robe?

The autumn of life

Growing old was not something to look forward to in Pompeii; old women were the target of cruel caricatures by painters and mosaicists, who especially liked to portray them as characters in plays by Menander. Here, an old woman, with hollow eyes and a wrinkled face, and two younger, rather plain peasant women – probably mother and daughter – are sitting at a table, on which are an incense-burner and a laurel wreath. The old woman is about to prepare a charm; she has been asked a question and waves her hands in the air, then drinks from a goblet of wine. The young woman on the far left wrings her hands in despair, while the servant, on the right, stands quietly by. Aged fortune-tellers could turn the credulity of ordinary folk to good advantage.

This wealthy Pompeian lady, whose whole life seems to have been devoted to the carefree enjoyment of luxury, did not escape the dramatic events that struck the city. Her house was badly shaken by the earthquake of AD 62. Yet she remained calm in the face of adversity and decided to pay for repairs to her home by letting part of it, which she had converted into public baths, shops, and a *thermopolium*. Julia Felix epitomizes a class of women who owed their independence to large inherited fortunes, but who did not seek to play any economic role in city life.

Eumachia, businesswoman and priestess, displays her wealth

Another woman who occupied a position of unusual importance in Pompeian society was Eumachia. She was born into an old Pompeian family, the Eumachii, who owned vineyards and brickworks, as well as playing an important part in municipal affairs; one member of the *gens*, Lucius Eumachius Festus, had been an aedile in AD 32. Eumachia was the owner of a vast edifice on the forum, on the corner of the Via dell'Abbondanza, measuring 60 m x 40 m; over the two entrances to the building an inscription reads: 'Eumachia, daughter of Lucius, priestess of the people, in her own name and in that of her son Numistrius Fronto, built this entrance hall, a cryptoporticus and a portico with her own money, and dedicated them to the honour of Augustan Concord and Piety'.

By chance, in the course of the excavations a statue of Eumachia was found here, which had been erected by the corporation of the fullers, in honour of their generous patroness; this seems to confirm the

Ground plan of the building of Eumachia
The facade opens onto the portico of the forum, while at the back the building leads into the Via dell'Abbondanza.

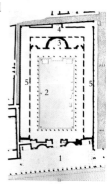

Longitudinal section
1. Portico of the forum
2. Colonnade
3. Apse and statue of Livia
4. Gallery containing statue of Eumachia

1

assumption that the building was used as a wool market, an activity to which it would have been well suited. Tables and other fittings required by the traders could have been set up either in the open courtyard or under the colonnade, while the covered gallery, or cryptoporticus, which ran round three sides of the building, could have been locked up after working hours to protect the merchandise stored there.

Quite apart from its suitability for commercial purposes, the building of Eumachia is striking for the monumentality and beauty of its architecture. The facade, consisting of a two-storey colonnade, blends

Cross-section
2. Colonnade framing the entrance to the apse
5. Gallery

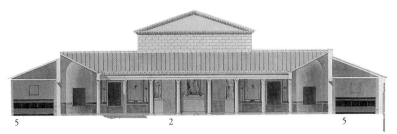

5   2   5

in with the new colonnade of the forum. The supports and lintel of the main entrance are ornamented with a superb carved marble frieze; niches in the facade and others inside the building were designed to display statues of the emperors – Tiberius and Drusus, no doubt – while inscriptions celebrate the lives of Aeneas and Romulus. The general effect is reminiscent of the Augustan forum in Rome. Inside, a large courtyard surrounded by a two-storey colonnade is terminated by an end wall with

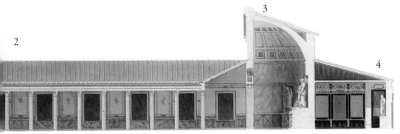

3

2

4

three semicircular apses; the central apse, fronted by two ornate columns, displays a statue of Concordia Augusta holding a cornucopia. The Concordia Augusta is a personification of the Empress Livia, wife of Augustus, and it celebrates the emotional union between her and her son Tiberius, after her illness of AD 22. By erecting this statue, Eumachia demonstrated her loyalty to the emperor and to his mother, indicating that she took their family relationship as a model in her own life. It is also possible that, as a public priestess, Eumachia celebrated the cult of this Livia–Ceres figure.

This building reveals the wealth and power of the Eumachii, as well as their pride, in that they dared to erect in Pompeii a small-scale imitation of the imperial forum. Ostentatious in life, they were no less so in death, as we can see from the impressive sepulchre that Eumachia had constructed for herself and her kin, *sibi et suis*.

The women who ran businesses and bars, or who lived by their charms...

The wives of craftsmen and traders were often responsible for running the shop; in a painting of the baker Terentius Neo, the woman at his side holds a stylus and writing tablet for drawing up the accounts. In the shop of M. Vecilius Verecundus, a major manufacturer of cloth and felt, it is his wife who is shown sitting at the counter, while an elegantly dressed young man chooses a pair of slippers from the cupboards full of merchandise that line the walls.

It was often women who ran the inns and bars, which were frequented by a somewhat coarse

The acanthus scrolls that decorate the lintel of the building of Eumachia are inhabited by small animals, snails, rats and birds, reminding us of the Romans' taste for naturalism. The statue of Eumachia (below), on the other hand, reveals Greek influence.

clientele. One of these inn-keepers was Valeria Hedone, whose language was colourful and whose tone, strident; even her surname, which is Greek for 'pleasure', implies a great deal about her. Shamelessly, she cries her wares: 'Handsome soldier, drink here for just one as; for two you can drink better, and for four have some really good Falernian wine.' If a brawl broke out between her dice-playing customers, she could be tough and have the trouble-makers thrown

This woman, possibly a baker's wife, is typical of a class of ambitious women who played an important role in Pompeian life. In her hand she holds a jointed writing tablet, probably used for recording the accounts.

into the street without a moment's hesitation. Close by, in a 'specialist' bar, a lady called Asellina was in charge of a whole cohort of girls who offered their charms for a modest price in the winding streets of old Pompeii. Palmyra the Oriental, Aglae the Greek, Maria the Jewess, Zmyrina the Exotic: the names of those who inhabited the Lupanar are familiar to us from graffiti which proclaim their various specialities. The faces of many Pompeian women have been lost in the blank anonymity of their work. Among the working women of Pompeii were the bakery assistants Statia and Petronia, the women in the fulling mills, like Specula, who was employed to brush and shear the cloth, and all the many domestic servants, kitchen maids and chambermaids, who revolved around the mistress of the house.

Rich Pompeian ladies would have spent much of their time surrounded by a crowd of servants (below), deciding what to wear and having their hair and make-up done. Only a servant would have knelt on the floor (below right), but this woman's pose remains graceful nonetheless. Some women of the period wrote poetry; the young girl in the roundel (right) bites the end of her stylus as she meditates, no doubt searching for inspiration.

The pattern of daily life was recorded by the sundials and water clocks, or *clepsydrae*, which measured the passage of time. They fixed the hours of the working day and indicated when the tribunals were in session, when performances would begin at the theatre, or games at the amphitheatre; they measured the time for lovers' meetings, business dinners and banquets with friends.

CHAPTER 5

A LIFE OF LEISURE

The spectacle of violent games drew the Pompeian crowds. They idolized the boxing champions, as well as the heroes of the amphitheatre, who paraded wearing their ceremonial helmets.

In the bars a favourite pastime was dice-playing, but quarrels were a frequent occurrence.

These two athletes have just been proclaimed the winners of games held at the *palaestra*. The one in the foreground, his hair tied back with a headband, raises a glass vase to celebrate his victory; the second athlete, behind him, wears a laurel wreath around his head as a mark of success.

Everyone in Pompeii tried, as far as his means would allow, to make time for *otium* – that is, leisure rather than laziness, the opposite of *negotium*, or work, with all its cares and worries.

Sport, the citizens' favourite activity, developed their strength and skills

As early as the 5th century BC, members of the Samnite aristocracy were training at the Samnite *palaestra*, or sports ground. This was far too small for the Romans, who constructed the large *palaestra*, a vast, multi-purpose campus, which was at once a training area, a place for walking, a parade ground for the barracks, a slave market and a cockfighting arena. The huge rectangular area – 141 m by 107 m, or more than 15,000 square metres – was bounded by a wall as solid as the defences of a *castrum*; on the inside, three raised porticoes surrounded the courtyard, in the centre of which there was a swimming pool. The perfectly straight rows of plane trees planted here provide a

On the table lies a purse full of money which will go to the owner of the winning cockerel. Before the fight, spectators placed bets in an atmosphere of feverish excitement.

striking example of the kind of arboreal architecture that has been found in other gardens of the city.

Keen amateurs came here to throw the discus, practise the long jump with weights in their hands or to wrestle. Certain types of sport had a more military flavour: running in full armour, parading on horseback while skilfully executing the complicated manoeuvres of the *ludus Troiae*, or Trojan game. In this way young men prepared themselves mentally and physically for their future role in city life.

After physical exercise, baths were essential for the hygiene of young and old alike

The importance of the baths can be gauged from their number – three for the city of Pompeii alone – and from their location in the busiest and most accessible areas of the city: the Stabian Baths at the Holconius crossroads, the Forum Baths at the junction of the Via del Foro and the Via di Nola, and the Central Baths at the crossing of the *decumanus maximus* and the *cardo maximus*. These three establishments allow us to follow the development of bath architecture from the Samnite period, through the city's early days as a Roman colony, when the Forum Baths were constructed, right up to the time of the eruption, when the Central Baths were still unfinished.

The central block in all cases comprised the hot bath (*caldarium*), the warm steamroom (*tepidarium*) and the cold bath (*frigidarium*), arranged along a single east–west axis. It opened onto the *palaestra* courtyard, which had a portico running round three

The *tepidarium* of the Forum Baths (far left) was heated by a large bronze brazier ornamented with calves' heads, the symbol of the donor, Nigidius Vaccula. The walls have niches set into them, which are divided by atlantes, supporting an elaborate cornice carved with acanthus scrolls. The ceiling is decorated with stucco panels.

Light enters through a round window over the wash basin in the *caldarium* (left), in accordance with the recommendations of the Roman architect Vitruvius, while a rectangular light-well illuminates the rest of the room.

Forum Baths

THE MEN'S BATH
I *Apodyterium* (changing room)
II *Frigidarium*
III *Tepidarium*
IV *Caldarium*
THE WOMEN'S BATH
1 *Apodyterium*
2 *Frigidarium*
3 *Tepidarium*
4 *Caldarium*

sides, the fourth being taken up by an ornamental pool and the service quarters. In the Stabian Baths, the inclusion of a women's bath, separated from that of the men, meant that a sundial had to be used to regulate the opening times for men and women. The same separation of men and women can be found at the Forum Baths. The *frigidarium* was a circular, vaulted room; the entrance hall and undressing room, or *apodyterium*, were also vaulted, their ceilings covered with octagonal and circular panels decorated with stucco.

A large staff were responsible for seeing to customers' needs. Some helped the disabled to climb the steps of the baths or to lower themselves into the cold pool; others helped to shower those who were not allowed to bathe. After the bath it was the turn of the hair-removers, perfumers and masseurs (who were mainly blacks). These moments of relaxation were all part of the delights of living in Pompeii, and with the construction of the Central Baths, more and more Pompeians could devote themselves to bathing. In the bathing establishment of M. Crassus Frugi, there were even salt-water baths, though these were reserved for a privileged clientele.

Pompeians had a choice of entertainment: theatre, Odeon or amphitheatre

The theatre, which dates from the Samnite period, *c.* 200 BC, is both the oldest and the largest of the places of entertainment. In its horseshoe-shaped *cavea*, or auditorium, four semicircular walls support the great bank of earth which is covered by tiers of stone seats capable of holding five thousand spectators. To the south of the theatre lay a garden

In the *caldarium* of the Forum Baths (below), where the golden yellow walls are decorated with elegant red porphyry pilasters, visitors to the establishment passed from the hot bath to the *labrum*, a marble bowl from which sprang a jet of cold water. This *caldarium* is also shown in the 19th-century engraving below right. The same engraver recorded the *tepidarium* of the Forum Baths (above right), with its elaborate stucco decoration.

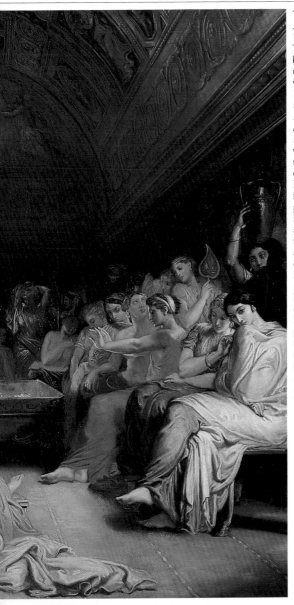

Like many of his contemporaries, in 1853 the French painter Théodore Chassériau bowed to the fashion for the antique with this work entitled *Tepidarium; the Room where the Women of Pompeii Came to Relax and Dry Themselves after Bathing*. However, the women are actually shown in the *tepidarium* of the men's bath at the Forum Baths! Apart from this anomaly, the painter was careful to reproduce the archaeological details with considerable accuracy. He quite correctly introduced into the scene the *tepidarium*'s bronze brazier and seats decorated with calves' heads (see p. 96). The painting evokes the same atmosphere of languid sensuality as the more famous *Bain Turc* by Ingres and Delacroix's *Femmes d'Alger*.

Back-stage, actors are busy choosing their masks and costumes.

From their position on the terraced seats of the *cavea*, the spectators had a perfect view down onto the stage. The stage shown below dates from the reconstruction of the large theatre carried out under Nero, between AD 63 and 68. It was dominated by a richly decorated stage wall, with a vast, semicircular niche in the centre, flanked on each side by a rectangular niche.

surrounded by an Ionic colonnade, where pleasant walks could be enjoyed during the intervals. This vast open space was linked to the Via Stabiana and, by a wide flight of steps, to the Triangular Forum.

Between AD 63 and 68, a Roman-style *scenae frons* was built. Composed of a large, semicircular central niche flanked by two rectangular recesses, it had three openings cut into it: the royal entrance and two other doorways which were conventionally supposed to lead, on one side, to the city, and on the other, to the countryside. Behind the stage was a trench designed to hold the curtain that was lowered at the beginning of each performance; contrary to modern theatrical convention, the raising of the curtain signified the end of the show.

A second cultural venue, the Odeon, was built under Sulla. This indoor theatre was intended for musical performances, poetry recitals and lectures. The roofing of this structure, necessary for acoustical reasons, must have represented a considerable technical challenge; this explains why the *cavea,* which forms a perfect circle, seems very steep in comparison to the large theatre. The thirty-nine tiers of seats made of tufa comfortably accommodated 1300 spectators, who could move around the theatre with ease.

In the Odeon, elegant decorative details help to alleviate the plainness of the materials and the severe lines of the architecture. Tufa atlantes support each end of the back wall of the *cavea*, and griffins' claws are carved on the wall separating the *ima cavea* from the *media cavea*.

Twenty thousand spectators go to watch the games at the amphitheatre

The amphitheatre, which dates from the same period as the Odeon (*c.* 75 to 70 BC), was built in the form of an ellipse, backing onto a stretch of the city wall. Thirty-five rows of seats provided space for twenty thousand spectators, who took their places according to a strict social hierarchy, the important citizens occupying the lower rows. A whole society assembled here to acclaim the heroes of the games.

1

The theatre quarter: longitudinal section

"On my first visit to Pompeii in 1857, I was struck by the beauty of the city's ruins.... In addition to its great charm and novelty, the quarter around the theatres and the Triangular Forum offered me a series of buildings and monuments, almost all of which had preserved clear indications of their original decoration. The quarter includes a public square, known as the Triangular Forum, in the middle of which can still be found traces of a Greek temple.... a large and a small theatre; quarters for soldiers, a public market; a temple dedicated to Isis...; private houses, a city gate and the ramparts complete the ensemble."

Paul-Emile Bonnet

Paul-Emile Bonnet's drawings reflect the actual condition of the theatre quarter in 1859 and his suggested reconstruction of it.

1. The gladiators' barracks
2. A side view of the stage wall, showing the means of access to it
3. The *parados*, or entrance for the chorus
4. The *cavea*
5. The Samnite *palaestra*

5

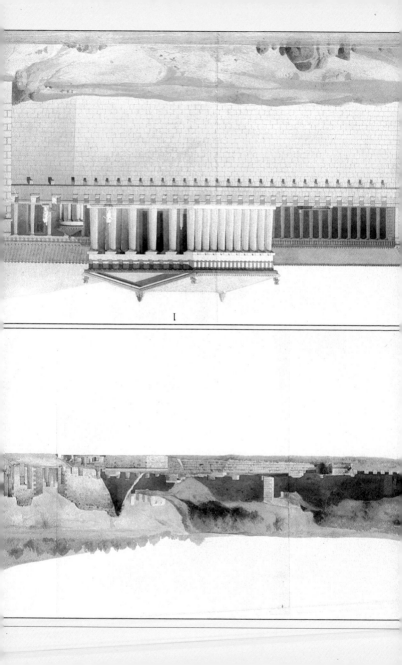

I

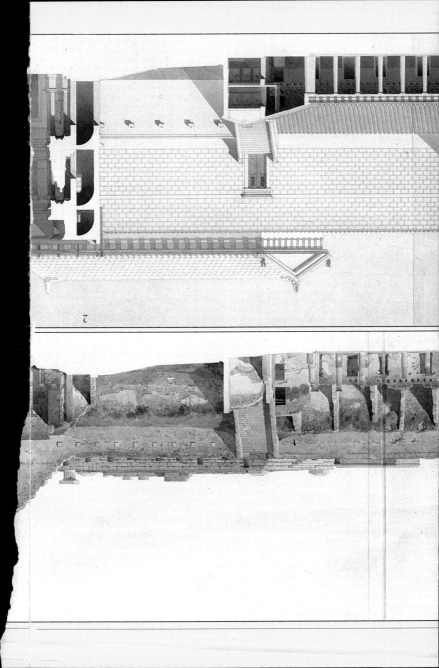

"These various buildings stand on land that slopes gently towards the sea; the way in which they cluster together, rising one above and behind the other, must have created some very picturesque views in this area of the city."

Paul-Emile Bonnet

In the reconstruction below left of foldout, the outer wall is visible, together with two towers and the Stabian Gate. In both, the following buildings can be identified:

1 The Triangular Forum with the Doric temple, in front of which stands a beautiful *monopteros* surrounding a sacred well
2 The large theatre
3 The Odeon
4 The Stabian Gate

Left: the theatre quarter in its restored state.

Overleaf: a vertical section of the large theatre (detail from the reconstruction drawing in the foldout). This view demonstrates the division of the *ima cavea*, the *media cavea* and the *summa cavea*, which were placed one above the other. The whole was shaded from the sun by the *velum*, a large sheet attached to wooden posts and adjusted by cables.

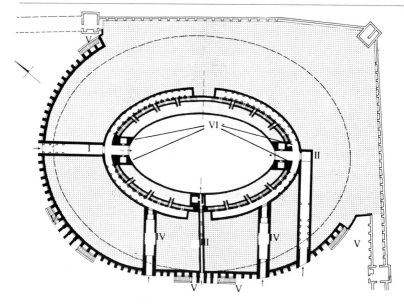

The organization of the games was in the hands of rich Pompeians, such as Cn. Alleius Nigidius Maius, who was proclaimed 'prince of the impresarios'. The aim was to get the highest number of pairs of gladiators to fight: perhaps thirty in five days, or forty in four days. The calendar was packed in the run-up to the hot summer months; games were held on 4, 8, 9, 10, 11, 12 and 20 April, and on 2, 12, 13, 14, 16 and 31 May. Games were also held in neighbouring towns such as Nola, Nocera and Pozzuoli in connection with regular feast-days, such as the Games of Apollo (6 – 13 July), or to commemorate special events, like the consecration of the Temple of Vespasian or the opening of the Archives.

This enthusiasm for the games increased still further under the empire, and after AD 62 the quadriporticus of the large theatre was converted into a barracks for the gladiators; individual cell rooms were constructed on two floors, while the courtyard was used for daily exercise. The gladiators tended to be professionals who had been taught combat techniques at specialist schools; the impresarios paid

Plan of the amphitheatre
I North axial gallery
II South axial gallery
III Gallery along the lesser axis
IV Corridors leading to the inner walkways
V Outer staircases
VI *Carceres* (rooms for the gladiators and animal cages)

To reduce the amount of earth-moving involved in the construction of the amphitheatre, the architects arranged the ellipse so that it would back onto a portion of the city wall. The building measures 140 x 105 m, and it encloses an arena 66.8 x 35.4 m.

large sums of money for their services. They were extraordinarily popular, no doubt because of a certain morbid fascination with men whose job it was to confront death every day – even though the public and magistrates often chose to spare the best gladiators, trained at the Capuan schools. They were also celebrated for their amorous exploits; the eruption of AD 79 surprised one wealthy, bejewelled Pompeian lady in a cell at the barracks, who was found lying dead beside her gladiator lover.

Gladiatorial combat was not the only spectacle to be seen at the amphitheatre. Other duels were held there: *venatio*, or fighting between men and lions, between wild and domesticated animals, or between lions and gazelles, often constituted the second half of the games. Although they

From either side of the amphitheatre on the main north–south axis, two corridors lead into the arena – though one is bent at a right-angle because of the city wall. A third corridor was probably used to remove dead animals and men. The spectators gained their seats either by the two corridors giving access to the internal walkways, or by the outer staircases which led to the upper levels.

This heavily armed gladiator of the *hoplomachus* type (left), with his helmet, greaves and dagger, suggests formidable efficiency in combat.

"At about the same time [AD 59], a trifling incident between the colonies of Nuceria and Pompeii provoked a terrible massacre; it arose at a gladiatorial show arranged by Livineius Regulus. During an exchange of taunts – characteristic of these disorderly country towns – abuse led to stone throwing, and then swords were drawn. The people of Pompeii, where the display was being held, came off best. Many Nucerians were taken home wounded and mutilated; many bereavements, too, were suffered by parents and children. The emperor instructed the Senate to investigate the affair, and the Senate passed it to the consuls. When they reported back, the Senate debarred Pompeii from holding any similar gathering for ten years.... Livineius and others held responsible for the disorders were exiled."

Tacitus
Annals, XIV, 17

The paintings round the podium of the amphitheatre enable us to follow the preparations for combat made by the various types of gladiator, from those on horseback (top left) to the *retiarii*, who fought with a net and trident. The centre painting serves as a reminder that the amphitheatre was also a hunting ground, where men fought bulls or wild boar, and where dogs fought boar, stags and deer.

glorified cruelty and indulged a taste for blood, these duels also demonstrated the courage of the combatants in their struggles with the ferocious wild beasts.

In contrast to these brutal and disturbing pastimes, the theatre offered Pompeians a more refined form of entertainment

Although Pompeians enjoyed both pure comedy and pure tragedy, they did not object to being moved from laughter to tears within the same performance. They loved the pathos and rhetoric, lyricism and

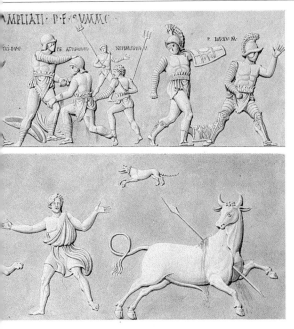

Scenes of gladiatorial combat, engraved on the handle of this bronze strigil used in the baths (below), indicate the important role played by the games in the leisure time of Pompeians.

violence of plays by the tragic poet Seneca, but they enjoyed still more comedies of manners based on works by Menander. These held up a mirror to contemporary society, reflecting the everyday lives of the rich bourgeoisie, in which slaves and freedmen played an increasingly important role. In the house that is named after him, Menander is shown seated, crowned with a laurel wreath and holding a scroll of papyrus on which is written: 'Menander was the first to write a New Comedy in four acts'.

Especially popular with the public were farces that caricatured all kinds of familiar professions. Coalmerchants, fortune-tellers, painters, potters: anyone could become the target of the comic writer. There was also a great vogue for new forms of entertainment: mime, in which the burlesque plots often revolved around adultery, and pantomime, silent productions based on dance and gesture.

Only the Odeon held itself aloof from this move towards popular taste; the select few went there to

applaud the latest fashionable poet, who, wearing a laurel crown and a mask, would declaim his most recent verses. With this exception, the shows put on in the theatres were on the same level as the spectacles of the amphitheatre.

Higher cultural entertainment appears to have been restricted to schools and the esoteric studies pursued by a handful of learned individuals in the privacy of their well-stocked libraries. The lower classes demanded light-hearted drama, broad farce that could make them roar with laughter, or bloody games that simultaneously excited and satisfied their instinct for violence.

Followed by a poor dwarf, a woman accompanies on her flute the dance of two men, one of whom plays the cymbals, while the other beats a tambourine. This mosaic illustrates a scene from a play by Menander.

A slave insults a young couple by making the sign of horns – the Neapolitan gesture *par excellence.* The man is trying to protect the young woman, who seems terrified. The slave has grey hair and wears a heavy cloak draped in the manner of a bourgeois. The cloak is decorated with a fringe – a sign of wealth – and this figure may therefore represent one of Menander's heroes, a freedman named Pappos. His adventures caused amusement amongst both slaves and freedmen.

At home or in the street, in private or in public, Pompeians were always in the presence of the gods. They worshipped them at regular hours in the many shrines and temples of the city, but they also devoted a good deal of their time to them when they returned to the intimacy of their own homes.

CHAPTER 6

OF GODS AND MEN

Pompeii 'the devout' made sacrifices day and night to its own native gods, as well as to exotic foreign deities. Bacchus (left) was worshipped everywhere. The Egyptian goddess Isis received praises from her faithful followers during the ceremony of the lustral waters (opposite), held daily at half past two in the afternoon.

The most important cult: the triad of Hercules, Bacchus and Venus, protectors of the vine

These three divinities were often allowed a place in the *lararium*, the shrine at which the head of the household would daily worship his ancestors, or Lares, surrounded by the members of his family and his slaves. The *lararia* tend to feature paintings of Hercules, the legendary founder of Pompeii, while in small domestic shrines and courtyard gardens, Dionysiac statuettes, theatrical masks and busts of

Venus Pompeiana, draped in azure blue and wearing a golden crown, stands in a quadriga drawn by elephants, holding an olive branch. She represents triumphant Fortuna, who well deserves the palm and crown offered to her by two small cupids.

Bacchus glorify the god of wine. Pompeians also rendered homage to Venus, whom they addressed as *Venus Pompeiana*; as the city's official goddess, she was expected to bring them good luck and prosperity. Closely associated with Bacchus, the god of wine, she was an agrarian deity whose cult would later be combined with that of Ceres. She occupied a place of honour in the *lararia* and reigned over a large sanctuary close to the forum.

Two figures stand on either side of Venus' chariot: on the left is Fortuna, mistress of the world, bearing a cornucopia; on the right, the public Genius of Pompeii holds out a *patera*, or ceremonial dish.

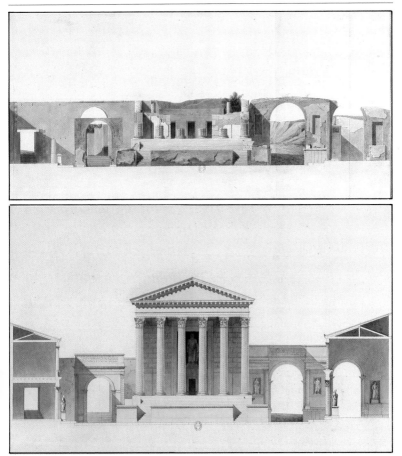

Jupiter, Juno, Minerva: worship of the Capitoline Triad symbolized support for Roman sovereignty

These three deities enjoyed great popularity from the time of Sulla's founding of the Roman colony of Pompeii. The Temple of Capitoline Jupiter dominates the forum; in the *cella*, the house of the god, a triple pedestal was designed to hold the three divine statues. Priests administered the official cult, but Jupiter, Juno and Minerva were also worshipped in private houses.

The Temple of the Capitoline Triad, where Jupiter, Juno and Minerva were worshipped, has a facade of six columns, each 8.4 m high, supporting an impressive pediment. To the right of the temple stands the Arch of Tiberius.

The priests and priestesses of Isis wore white linen robes, shoes made of palm leaves or papyrus, and a headband decorated with the uraeus serpent, or cobra. The priest (left) carries a bowl filled with lustral water, which he sprinkles about with an aspergillum. The priestess presents him with an *oenochoe*, or wine flask. The priest below is shaking a sistrum, or rattle, a form of musical instrument.

Isis, the foreign goddess

Roman religion had always proved very tolerant of foreign deities; through their trade links with the Sicilian ports and with Delos in the Cyclades the Pompeians discovered the Egyptian gods and introduced their worship into Campania. Their cult was particularly popular amongst the lower classes, the slaves and families of freedmen who made up the staff of the great houses. Even after they had been freed, the descendants of freedmen and former slaves continued to display their devotion to these gods, a devotion that the aristocracy later came to share.

The cult gradually took hold amongst the upper classes of the Pompeian population, eventually becoming the city's semi-official religion. The son of a freedman restored the Temple of Isis after its complete destruction by the earthquake of AD 62. Who was the generous patron? None other than a six-year-old child, N. Popidius Celsinus – assisted, admittedly, by his father. It was a gesture that opened the doors of the municipal council to him; but it is still proof of the enthusiasm for Isis felt by the city's aristocratic classes. At the houses of Loreius

Tiburtinus and Julia Felix the garden contains a shrine dedicated to Isis, statuettes of pharaohs and Egyptian deities; important citizens like Cn. Poppaeus Habitus worshipped the goddess with great fervour.

In the Temple of Isis daily ceremonies were performed in her name. Before sunrise, the image of the goddess was presented to her adoring followers, who gathered in front of the temple to thank her in their prayers and to shake the *sistrum* in her honour. The worshippers remained seated, deep in prayer and contemplation, until after sunrise; the service ended with an invocation to the newly risen sun. At two o'clock in the afternoon a second ceremony was held for the adoration of consecrated water.

In addition to these daily rites, Isis was the focus for elaborate festivities, the most important of which was the *navigium Isidis*, celebrated on 5 March; as the patroness of sailors, it was appropriate that she should be honoured at a time of year when they were beginning to set sail once more, after the winter. The second festival, Isia (13 – 16 November), commemorated Isis' discovery of the body of Osiris. Public joy was translated into secret initiation rites undergone by the servants of Isis, who renounced their past life and, through this rebirth, committed themselves to leading a purer life in the future.

A traveller, recognizable by his short tunic and long staff, asks the Sybil to provide him with a philtre. It is natural that, as a stranger to the place, he should seek magical assistance before entering the city.

The Villa of the Mysteries: scenes from the myth of Dionysos

In the Villa of the Mysteries, a suburban mansion not far from Pompeii, an elaborate fresco decorates a room discreetly hidden at the centre of the house. It is dedicated to Dionysos, the universally beneficent god. Twenty-nine figures and numerous scenes can be made out, running continuously round the room. The main protagonists are Dionysos himself – indicated by his *thyrsus,* a staff entwined with vine leaves and ivy – and Semele, his mother; they can be seen embracing in the centre of the lower panel (left). On either side of this central image, two myths unfold: that of Dionysos and that of Semele, each of which is mirrored by the life of a priestess.

The Villa of the Mysteries: scenes from the myth of Semele

The woman at her toilet (above) symbolizes Semele preparing for her marriage to Zeus. The portion of the fresco shown opposite develops the allegory of Semele's pregnancy and the birth of Dionysos. For a fuller interpretation of these scenes, see pp. 186-91.

Not all Pompeians were so spiritually elevated, however, and some went to any lengths to ward off the evil eye – magic urns, ghostly hands. This distinctive brand of religious sensibility derived from Bacchic rites. In the 70s of the 1st century the new Christian religion had yet to reach the people of Pompeii.

Pompeians recognized only one god on earth: the emperor

The imperial cult transcended all other cults, and all divine qualities were attributed to the emperor. As a descendant of Venus, the lover of Mars and mother of Romulus, the emperor inevitably drew all the divine triads into his own orbit. Thus, the college of slaves and freedmen who honoured Mercury and Maia, the *ministri mercuri et maiae*, became known between 14 and 2 BC as the *ministri augusti mercuri et maiae*, and after 2 BC simply as that of the *ministri augusti*.

In the centre of the courtyard of the Temple of Vespasian, a white marble altar bears a scene of ritual sacrifice associated with the imperial cult. The priest, his head covered by a fold of his toga, pours a libation; he may represent the Emperor Vespasian himself, in his role as the supreme pontiff. Two *lictores*, a flute-player and two young boys bring the sacred implements, while the sacrificial bull is led to the altar by the executioner and his assistant.

By associating himself with all things divine, the emperor offered every citizen the opportunity of worshipping him, regardless of ethnic or social differences. The freedmen, who played an important role in economic life, formed the college of *augustales*. They took on responsibility for the street shrines to the Lares of the Crossroads, the *lares compitales*, later known as the Augustan Lares, organizing the same ceremonies as the *vicomagistri* (area magistrates) in Rome.

An elaborate hierarchy composed of priests and priestesses, *augustales* and *ministri*, pledged themselves to the emperor. The forum celebrates this imperial glory through its statues and triumphal arches. The fact that space was set aside for the imperial cult can come as a surprise in certain contexts: there is a chapel in the market (*macellum*); in the Temple of the Lares; the Temple of Vespasian; the building of Eumachia; even in the large *palaestra*, where each young man had to perform propitiatory rites before exercising. This syncretism is most clearly expressed in the Temple of Apollo, where the cult was directed towards Apollo and Diana, to Mercury and Maia, and therefore, inevitably, to the emperor. Gradually, the triads lost favour and were replaced everywhere by the imperial monad.

Private religion

Pompeians devoted a fairly substantial portion of their free time to religious observance in their own homes, where, as in the Villa of the Mysteries, the decoration sometimes evokes a higher world that only the initiated are permitted to enter. The vitality of private religion is clear from the care with which the *lararia* in certain houses were restored and embellished after the earthquake of AD 62. Pompeii was a pious city, but not a bigoted one, in which each individual was free to express his or her own spiritual preferences through respect for the imperial religion, which pervaded all that was sacred.

Like the houses, the streets in Pompeii belonged to the gods; the Lares were often depicted on the surface of the walls. This shrine in the House of the Vettii takes the form of a classical temple facade, with a pediment supported by two columns.

On the rear wall, a Genius dressed in a toga is flanked by two Lares, who have the appearance of young men; wearing short, loose tunics, they raise high their drinking horns. At the bottom of the *lararium,* a great, many-coiled serpent with a crested head symbolizes the male ancestor, protector of the household, whom these libations are intended to placate.

Though they were blessed by the goddess of love, Pompeians did not worship Venus alone, nor did they lead carefree lives entirely free from the fear of death. The cemeteries just outside the city gates were an ever-present reminder of mortality, of the law that applies to all humanity, blindly striking young and old alike.

CHAPTER 7
LOVE AND DEATH
IN POMPEII

Even in the happiest moments of life, Pompeians were never wholly free from thoughts of death. No one was more aware than they of how short was the time for living, loving and dying.

No other city in the Roman world has played the part of love's messenger better than Pompeii. Venus, in all her many guises, ruled supreme there. Alongside the *Venus Pompeiana*, we find the *Venus Marina*, or Venus of the Shell, carelessly revealing her exquisite naked form. Elsewhere, she appears in a more discreetly erotic context, in an allegory of the love of Mars and Venus.

Inspired by the nearby sea, Pompeians honoured the *Venus Marina* (above), whose shell is drawn along by cupids, while a favourable breeze swells the veil above her head.

Meanwhile, the earthly Venus manifested her power in the quarters of ill-repute, in the lupanars and dark corners. Graffiti covering the facades of houses, shops and public buildings reveal a people who talked openly of love. We find crude remarks about amorous prowess, advice from girls skilled at their trade, memories of the two or five asses left on the counter next to the lamp with an erotic motif, the names and nicknames of pimps and procuresses, of boys and girls who prostituted themselves to all-comers, and colourful illustrations in the half-light of cells depicting the techniques of experienced whores. Elsewhere, an obscene Priapus or a scene of bestial coupling can be found side by side with idyllic images of romantic love: Hylas assailed by the nymphs, Narcissus at the fountain, Hero and Leander.... In the *triclinium* of the House of the Vettii, for example, panels depict pairs of mythical and legendary lovers: Perseus and Andromeda, Apollo and Daphne, Dionysos and Ariadne.

In Pompeii it is hard to avoid the clichéd image of the loves of Mars and Venus. Sometimes the two deities provocatively display their naked forms, but more often they are shown correctly dressed, rather like a bourgeois couple. Here, Mars, in military dress, has not yet removed his helmet, lance and breastplate, while Venus is swathed in a long tunic covered by a light cloak. The hand of Mars, straying over Venus' breast, is the only clue to the amorous significance of the scene.

Pompeians were very fond of erotic images, depicting either the loves of the gods or Priapic prowess. The sight of the figure (far left) weighing a huge phallus never fails to arouse the interest of visitors to the House of the Vettii. Placed in the entrance hall, the scene had an apotropaic intent, the idea being that such a sight would disarm the antique visitor, thus cleansing his spirit of any evil designs he might have had.

The poetic muse spices her song with amorous outpourings

Pompeians could produce a charming, discreetly allusive poem to match any occasion, no matter how improper. The lover hurrying to meet the object of his affections rails against the delay imposed by the mule-driver's thirst: 'If you were the one suffering the fires of love, muleteer, you would be in more of a hurry to see Venus. I love a young and handsome boy; I beg you, spur on your mules.... You've finished your drink, let's go; take up the reins and shake them. Take me to Pompeii where my sweet love is waiting.'

Elsewhere, Venus is invoked to further a man's pursuit of love: 'Do not forget me, dear mistress, I beg you, by Venus Fisica!' The goddess is also called upon to assist the lover in wreaking mortal vengeance: 'I beg you, let my rival perish!' But the disappointed lover, cruelly defeated, turns on the goddess,

threatening to tear her limb from limb and to return her false-hearted treachery blow for blow.

In general, however, the Pompeian lover is calm and gentle, claiming only the right to love: 'Lovers are like bees; their lives are sweet as honey.' The art of love is in some respects an art of living: 'Long live lovers! Death to those who know not how to love! Double death to those who hinder love!'

Pompeian women were not just objects of fleeting desire, but precious, life-long companions

Ever since the age of Nero, a disillusioned society, infected with world-weariness, had been searching for something to give life new meaning; in the virtues of the Pompeian wife it found a fresh ideal. The torments of Ixion and of Dirce, for example, stressed the value of self-discipline and submission to the will of the gods. In the House of the Vettii (VI, 15, 1), the mural painters contrasted the legitimate love of Peleus and Thetis with more unhappy, illicit affairs, and offered divine couples as a model for earthly lovers.

By contrast, this painting from the rear kitchen of the House of the Vettii, a scene of amorous dalliance with a servant, takes sexual realism fairly far. The master of the house is exercising his 'rights' over a young servant girl, in a plainly decorated room that contrasts sharply with the sumptuous cushions and covers of the room top left.

Faced with this Venus (left), who emphasizes her natural charms with golden netting, a young Priapus betrays his excitement.

The Street of Tombs, by Samuel Palmer.

"It's a big mistake to have nice houses just for when you're alive and not worry about the one we have to live in for much longer."
Petronius, *Satiricon*

Love inspires feelings of piety, reverence for gods and respect for men, whether living or dead

The roads leading to Pompeii, lined with ostentatious tombs, are like so many streets of the dead; and yet the image of death is not a distressing one. Amongst the tombs and the cypress trees that shade them, the shadow of death has no chill. The orchards in these cemeteries are in flower, and in the sunshine inscriptions and relief carvings glorify the names of magistrates and other citizens. Shops, inns and sumptuous country mansions stand amongst the tombs; life continues alongside death. Apart, perhaps, from the occasional funeral ceremony, a moving tribute paid to the defunct by relatives and friends, and the sobs of a mourning family breaking the stillness, nothing would have suggested sorrow in these streets, which, even today, invite the visitor to ponder and to remember.

The history of the city can be read in the inscriptions on the tombs; the burial grounds are the repository of past glories.

In the cemeteries we rediscover the social hierarchy of the living, as the aristocratic classes perpetuated the memory of their high offices and occupations. But these important citizens did not lie alone within their lofty tombs; the small niches in the burial vault held the bones of their relatives, while within the sepulchral wall were the more humble members of the household, whom they had fed and nurtured. An amphora or small urn was sufficient to hold the cremated remains of a slave or freedman; a stone was laid over the mouth of the buried amphora and pierced by a tube, through which libations could be poured. A stela, sometimes of marble, recorded the servant's name, and in the case of one of Livy's slaves, the marble was carved in the shape of a face, framed by braided hair. Peace reigned amongst the dead as it did amongst the living, and even in a society founded on slavery, death abolished class divisions.

The architecture of the funerary monuments is extremely varied, and many are striking for their majestic character. In the necropolis by the Herculaneum Gate stands the Tomb of the Istacidii, a circular temple surrounded by half-columns; the *tholos,* or vaulted chamber, composed of Ionic

columns, shelters statues of members of the family. The Tomb of Umbricius Scaurus, a wealthy manufacturer and dealer in *garum*, exhibits a decorative scheme inspired by the games held at the amphitheatre, showing gladiators and animals of the hunt.

The necropolis at the Nucerian Gate contains several monuments raised by women to the glory of their husbands: Veia Barchilla on behalf of Agrestinus Equitius Pulcher, or Eumachia's grandiose apse. Another interesting tomb is that constructed for her husband by Naevoleia Tyche, which carries a bas-relief showing a ship entering harbour.

A catastrophic eruption brings the death of Pompeii itself

The proud sepulchres and luxurious tombs cannot erase the memory of those who died in the summer of AD 79, who had as their shroud a layer of ash and pumice several metres thick.

Nothing could be more poignant than the dead discovered in 1961 close to the Nucerian Gate. Three families had clustered together under a roof to shelter from the hail of burning stones; they had died while trying to escape. One woman had fallen to her knees, pressing a cloth to her mouth to protect herself from the deadly fumes. Her husband must have watched her die, still holding the hand of their child, before finally succumbing himself.

DOCUMENTS

The history of Pompeii, of its
destruction and resurrection, in the
words of those who visited the city
and fell in love with it, who
understood its value and did their
best to preserve it for others.

The Campanian earthquake

The Roman philosopher Seneca, who was Nero's minister, is best known for his 'Dialogues', in which he discusses our knowledge of the workings of the human soul. Towards the end of his life he also became interested in the natural world. His 'Natural Questions' were intended as a scientific encyclopaedia covering all natural phenomena. The earthquake of AD 62, which destroyed several monuments in Pompeii, is described in this work.

Pompeii, the famous city in Campania, has been laid low by an earthquake which also disturbed all the adjacent districts. The city is in a pleasant bay, some distance from the open sea, and bounded by the shores of Surrentum and Stabiae on one side and of Herculaneum on the other; the shores meet there. In fact, it occurred in days of winter, a season which our ancestors used to claim was free from such disaster. This earthquake was on the Nones [5] of February, in the consulship of Regulus and Verginius. It caused great destruction in Campania, which had never been safe from this danger but had never been damaged, and time and again had got off with a fright. Also, part of the town of Herculaneum is in ruins, and even the structures which are left standing are shaky. The colony of Nuceria escaped destruction but still has much to complain about. Naples also lost many private dwellings but no public buildings, and was only mildly grazed by the great disaster; but some villas collapsed, others here and there shook without damage. To these calamities others were added: they say that a flock

Bas-relief showing the effects of the AD 62 earthquake on the various monuments of Pompeii. The Temple of the Capitoline Triad is clearly visible.

It is necessary to find solace for distressed people and to remove their great fear. Yet can anything seem adequately safe to anyone if the world itself is shaken, and its most solid parts collapse? Where will our fears finally be at rest if the one thing which is immovable in the universe and fixed, so as to support everything that leans upon it, starts to waver; if the earth loses the characteristic it has: stability? What hiding-place will creatures find, where will they flee in their anxiety, if fear arises from below and is drawn from the depths of the earth? There is panic on the part of all when buildings creak and give signs of falling. Then everybody hurls himself headlong outside, abandons his household possessions, and trusts to his luck in the outdoors. What hiding-place do we look to, what help, if the earth itself is causing the ruin, if what protects us, upholds us, on which cities are built, which some speak of as a kind of foundation of the universe, separates and reels?

Seneca
Naturales Quaestiones, VI

of hundreds of sheep was killed, statues were cracked, and some people were so shocked that they wandered about as if deprived of their wits. The thread of my proposed work, and the concurrence of the disaster at this time, requires that we discuss the causes of these earthquakes.

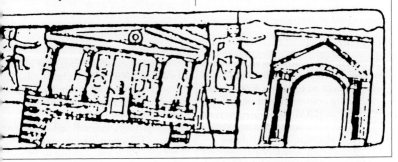

Pompeii, 24 August AD 79

Pliny the Younger, a friend of the Emperor Trajan (AD 97–117), was the nephew of Pliny the Elder, admiral of the Mediterranean fleet based at Misenum. The uncle was a man of encyclopaedic knowledge, who left thirty-seven books of a 'Natural History'. In AD 104 Pliny the Younger, who was a talented letter writer, wrote two letters (VI, 16 and 20) to the historian Tacitus (c. 55–120), in which he described the death of his uncle on the coast near Stabiae, and the emotions he felt as a young seventeen-year-old left behind at nearby Misenum, which must have been so similar to those experienced by the men and women of Pompeii on 24 August 79.

PLINE LE JEUNE.

Landon direx!

My uncle was stationed at Misenum in active command of the fleet. The ninth day before the Calends of September [24 August], in the early afternoon, my mother drew to his attention a cloud of unusual size and appearance. He had been out in the sun, had taken a cold bath, eaten a light lunch while lying down, and was then working at his books. He called for his shoes and climbed up to a place that would give him the best view of the phenomenon. It was not clear at that distance from which mountain the cloud was rising (it was afterwards known to be Vesuvius). Its general appearance can best be expressed as being like an umbrella pine, for it rose to a great height on a sort of trunk and then split off into branches, I imagine because it was thrust upwards by the first blast and then left unsupported as the pressure subsided, or else it was borne down by its own weight so that it spread out and gradually dispersed. In places it looked white, elsewhere blotched and dirty, according to the amount of soil and ashes it carried with it. My uncle's scholarly acumen saw at once that it was important enough for a closer inspection, and he ordered a boat to be made ready, telling me I could come with him if I wished. I replied that I preferred to go on with my studies, and as it happened he had himself given me some writing to do.

As he was leaving the house he was handed a message from Rectina, wife of Cascus, whose house was at the foot of the mountain, so that escape was impossible except by boat. She was terrified by the danger threatening her and implored him to rescue her from her fate. He changed his plans, and what he had begun in a spirit of enquiry he completed as a hero. He gave orders for the warships to be launched and went on board himself with the intention of bringing help to many more people besides Rectina, for this lovely stretch of coast was thickly populated.

He hurried to the place which everyone else was hastily leaving, steering his course straight for the danger zone. He was entirely fearless, describing each new movement and phase of the portent to be noted down exactly as he observed them. Ashes were already falling, hotter and thicker as the ships drew near, followed by bits of pumice and blackened stones, charred and cracked by the flames: then suddenly they were in shallow water, and the shore was blocked by the debris from the mountain. For a moment my uncle wondered whether

"Meanwhile, on Mount Vesuvius broad sheets of fire and leaping flames blazed at several points, their bright glare emphasized by the darkness of night."

to turn back, but when the helmsman advised this he refused, telling him that Fortune stood by the courageous and they must make for the home of Pomponianus at Stabiae. He was cut off there by the breadth of the bay (for the shore gradually curves round a basin filled by the sea) so that he was not as yet in danger, though it was clear that this would come nearer as it spread. Pomponianus had therefore already put his belongings on board ship, intending to escape if the contrary wind fell. The wind was of course full in my uncle's favour, and he was able to bring his ship in. He embraced his terrified friend, cheered and encouraged him, and thinking he could calm his fears by showing his own composure, gave orders that he was to be carried to the bathroom. After his bath he lay down and dined; he was quite cheerful, or at any rate he pretended he was, which was no less courageous.

Meanwhile on Mount Vesuvius broad sheets of fire and leaping flames blazed at several points, their bright glare emphasized by the darkness of night. My uncle tried to allay the fears of his companions by repeatedly declaring that these were nothing but bonfires left by the peasants in their terror, or else empty houses on fire in the districts they had abandoned.

Then he went to rest and certainly slept, for as he was a stout man his breathing was rather loud and heavy and could be heard by people coming and going outside his door. By this

Nothing could resist the rain of ash. After the houses, the temples succumbed: here, the Temple of Isis, the favourite Egyptian goddess of the Pompeians.

time the courtyard giving access to his room was full of ashes mixed with pumice-stones, so that its level had risen, and if he had stayed in the room any longer he would never have got out. He was wakened, came out and joined Pomponianus and the rest of the household, who had stayed up all night. They debated whether to stay indoors or take their chance in the open, for the buildings were now shaking with violent shocks, and seemed to be swaying to and fro as if they were torn from their foundations. Outside, on the other hand, there was the danger of falling pumice-stones, even though these were light and porous; however, after comparing the risks they chose the latter. In my uncle's case one reason outweighed the other, but for the others it was a choice of fears. As a protection against falling objects they put pillows on their heads tied down with cloths.

Elsewhere there was daylight by this time, but they were still in darkness, blacker and denser than any ordinary night, which they relieved by lighting torches and various kinds of lamps. My uncle decided to go down to the shore, to see at first hand whether it was possible to escape by sea; but they found the waves still wild and dangerous. There a sheet was spread on the ground for my uncle to lie down, and he called repeatedly for cold water, which he drank. Then the flames and smell of sulphur which heralded the approaching fire drove the others to take flight. Aroused, my uncle struggled to his feet, leaning on two slaves, but immediately collapsed. I assume that his breathing was impeded by the dense fumes, which blocked his windpipe – for it was constitutionally weak and narrow, and often inflamed.

When daylight returned – two days after the last time he had seen it – his body was found intact and uninjured, still fully clothed as in life. He looked more like a sleeper than a dead man.

You tell me that the letter in which, at your request, I described the death of my uncle has made you want to know what fears and even what dangers I myself experienced, having been left behind at Misenum (in fact, I had reached this point when I interrupted

On 11 May 1771, Vesuvius awoke once more. William Hamilton, the English ambassador, executed several watercolours of the subject.

myself). Although I tremble at the very memory, I will begin.

After my uncle's departure, I gave the rest of the day to study – the object which had kept me at home. Afterward I bathed, dined and retired to short and broken sleep. For several days we had experienced earth shocks, which hardly alarmed us as they are frequent in Campania. But that night they became so violent that it seemed the world was not only being shaken, but turned upside down. My mother rushed to my bedroom – I was just rising, as I intended to wake her if she was asleep. We sat down in the courtyard of the house, which separated it by a short distance from the sea. Whether from courage or inexperience (I was eighteen at the time), I called for a volume of Titus Livius and began to read, and even continued my notations from it, as if nothing were the matter. At this moment a friend of my uncle's arrived; he had just returned from Spain to see him. When he saw me sitting there, with my mother, when he saw me reading, he criticized me for my passivity and lack of concern; I continued to pay just as much enthusiastic attention to my book.

Though it was the first hour of the day, the light appeared to us still faint and uncertain. And though we were in an open place, it was narrow, and the buildings around us were so unsettled that the collapse of walls seemed a certainty. We decided to get out of town to escape this menace. The panic-stricken crowds followed us, in response to that instinct of fear which causes people to follow where others lead. In a long close tide they harassed and jostled us. When we were clear of the houses, we stopped, as we

encountered fresh prodigies and terrors. Though our carts were on level ground, they were tossed about in every direction, and even when weighted with stones could not be kept steady. The sea appeared to have shrunk, as if withdrawn by the tremors of the earth. In any event, the shore had widened, and many sea-creatures were beached on the sand. In the other direction loomed a horrible black cloud ripped by sudden bursts of fire, writhing snakelike and revealing sudden flashes larger than lightning.

Then my uncle's friend from Spain began to argue with great energy and urgency. 'If your brother,' he said, 'if your uncle is alive, he would want you to be saved; if he has perished, he would have wanted you to survive. Why, then, do you delay your escape?' We replied that we could not think of our own safety before finding out what had happened to him. Without a moment's further delay, he left us abruptly and escaped the danger in a frantic headless rush. Soon after, the cloud began to descend upon the earth and cover the sea. It had already surrounded and obscured Capreae [Capri], and blotted out Cape Misenum. My mother now began to beg, urge and command me to escape as best I could. A young man could do it; she, burdened with age and corpulence, would die easy if only she had not caused my death. I replied that I would not be saved without her. Taking her hand, I hurried her along. She complied reluctantly, and not without self-reproach for hindering me.

And now came the ashes, but at first sparsely. I turned around. Behind us, an ominous thick smoke, spreading over the earth like a flood, followed us. 'Let's go into the fields while we can still see the way,' I told my mother – for I was afraid that we might be crushed by the mob on the road in the midst of the darkness. We had scarcely agreed when we were enveloped in night – not a moonless night or one dimmed by cloud, but the darkness of a sealed room without lights. To be heard were only the shrill cries of women, the wailing of children, the shouting of men. Some were calling to their parents, others to their children, others to their wives – knowing one another only by voice. Some wept for themselves, others for their relations. There were those who, in their very fear of death, invoked it. Many lifted up their hands to the gods, but a great number believed there were no gods, and that this was to be the world's last, eternal night. Some added to the real danger with false or illusory terrors: 'In Misenum,' they would say, 'such and such a building has collapsed, and some other is in flames.' This might not be true, but it was believed.

A curious brightness revealed itself to us not as daylight but as approaching fire; but it stopped some distance from us. Once more, darkness and ashes, thick and heavy. From time to time we had to get up and shake them off for fear of being actually buried and crushed under their weight. I can boast that in so great a danger, I did not utter a single word or a single lamentation that could have been construed as weakness. I believed that one and all of us would perish – a wretched but strong consolation in my dying. But the darkness lightened, and then like smoke or cloud dissolved away. Finally a genuine daylight came; the sun shone, but pallidly, as in an eclipse. And then, before our terror-stricken gaze everything appeared changed – covered by a thick layer of ashes like an abundant snowfall.

We returned to Misenum, where we refreshed ourselves as best we could. We passed an anxious night between hope and fear – though chiefly the latter, for the earthquakes continued, and some pessimistic people were giving a ghoulish turn to their own and their neighbours' calamities by horrifying predictions. Even so, my mother and I – despite the danger we had experienced and the danger which still threatened – had no thought of leaving until we should receive some word of my uncle.

Such were the events; and you will read about them without the slightest intention of including the information in your works, as they are unworthy of history.... Adieu!

Pliny the Younger
Letters to Tacitus, VI, 16 and 20

A pioneer in Pompeii

Winckelmann was a self-taught enthusiast of classical art. Sent to Rome in 1757, he became a respected expert on antiquities. In 1762 he discovered the excavations at Herculaneum and Pompeii, and criticized the lack of organization that existed there.

Joh. Winkelmann.

A well dug for the prince of Elbeuf, at a small distance from his house, was the first thing, that gave occasion to the discovery they are now pursuing. The prince had built this house in order to make his constant residence in it. It lay behind the Franciscan convent, at the extremity of, and upon, a rock of lava near the sea. It afterwards fell into the hands of the house of Falletti of Naples, from whom the present king of Spain purchased it, in order to make a fishing seat of it. The well in question had been sunk near the garden of the barefooted Carmelites. To form it, they were obliged to dig through the lava to the live rock, where the workmen found, under the ashes of mount Vesuvius, three large clothed female statues. These the Austrian viceroy very justly laid claim to, and, keeping part of them in his hands, ordered them to Rome, where they were repaired. They were then presented to prince Eugene, who placed them in his gardens, at Vienna....

On the discovery of these antiquities, orders were given to the prince of Elbeuf, not to dig any further. Thirty years, however, were suffered to elapse, before any more notice was taken of them. At length, the present king of Spain, as soon as by the conquest of Naples he found himself in peaceable possession of it, chose Portici for his spring residence; and, as the well was still in being, ordered the works begun at the bottom of it to be continued, till they reached some buildings. This well still subsists. It runs down perpendicularly through the lava to the middle of the theatre, (the first building discovered,) which receives no light but by it. Here an inscription was found containing the name of Herculaneum, which, by giving room to guess what place they had hit upon, determined his majesty to proceed further.

The direction of this work was given to a Spanish engineer, called Roch Joachim Alcubierre, who had followed his majesty to Naples, and is now colonel, and chief of the body of engineers at Naples. This man, who (to use the Italian proverb), knew as much of antiquities, as the moon does of lobsters, has been, through his want of capacity, the occasion of many antiquities being lost. A single fact will be sufficient to prove it. The workmen having discovered a large public inscription (to what buildings it belonged, I can't say) in letters of brass two palms high; he ordered these letters to be torn from the wall, without first taking a copy of them, and thrown pell mell into a basket; and then presented them, in that condition, to the king. They were afterwards exposed for many years in the cabinet, where every one was at liberty to put them together as he pleased. Some imagined, they made these two words, IMP. AUG. I shall presently relate how a brazen four-horse chariot was served, by the same engineer's directions.

Don Roch having in time attained a higher rank, the superintendence and conduct of the works in question were committed to a Swiss officer, called Charles Weber, now a major; and it is to his good sense, that we are indebted for all the good steps since taken, to bring to light this treasure of antiquities. The first thing he did was, to make an exact map of all the subterraneous galleries, and the buildings they led to. This map he rendered still more intelligible, by a minute historical account of the whole discovery. The ancient city is to be seen in it as if freed from all the rubbish, with which it is actually incumbered. The inside of the buildings, the most private rooms, and the gardens, as well

The kings of Naples had a museum constructed close to their palace at Portici, and had the antique objects discovered at Herculaneum transported there for display with great solemnity.

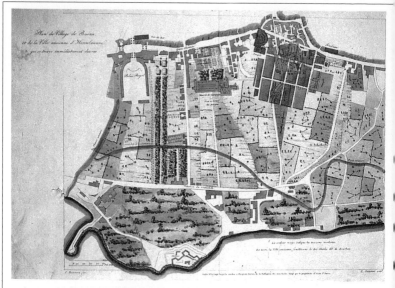

as the particular spots, where every thing taken out of them was found, appear in this map, just as they would, if they were laid quite bare. But nobody is permitted to see those drawings.

The happy issue of the works undertaken at Herculaneum proved a motive for opening the earth in other places; and the doing this soon enabled them to ascertain the situation of the ancient Stabia, and led them, at Pompeii, to the vast remains of an amphitheatre, built on a hill, part of which, however, had always been visible above ground. The diggings in these places proved far less expensive, than the diggings in Herculaneum, as there was no lava to dig through. The subterraneous works at Pompeii are those which promise most, for here they are not only sure of proceeding step by step in a great city, but have found out the principal street of it,

which runs in a strait line. But, notwithstanding all this certainty of their being able to find treasures unknown to our ancestors, the works for that purpose are carried on in a very slow and indolent manner; there being but fifty men, including the Algerine and Tunisian slaves, employed in all these subterraneous places. Great a city as Pompeii is known to have been, I, in my last journey, found but eight men at work on the ruins of it.

To compensate this neglect, the method observed in digging is such, that it is impossible the least spot should escape unnoticed. On both sides of one principal trench, carried on in a right line, the workmen alternately hollow out chambers, six palms in length, breadth, and height; removing the rubbish, as they proceed, from every one of these chambers, to the chamber opposite it, that was last hollowed out. This method is taken,

not only with a view of lessening the expence, but of supporting the earth over one chamber, with the rubbish taken out of another.

I know that strangers, particularly travellers, who can take but a cursory view of these works, wish, that all the rubbish was entirely removed, so as to give them an opportunity of seeing, as in the plan of which I have been speaking, the inside of the whole subterraneous city of Herculaneum. They are apt to impeach the taste of the Court, and of those who direct these works. But this is a mere prejudice, which a rational examination of the nature of the spot, and other circumstances, would soon conquer....

Those who have a mind to see the walls of ancient buildings formerly buried in the same manner, may satisfy their curiosity at Pompeii. But few persons, except Englishmen, have resolution enough to go so far on that account. At Pompeii the ground may be dug up, and turned topsy-turvy, without any risk, and at a small expence, the land lying over it being of little value. Formerly, indeed, it used to produce the most delicious wine; but that it now produces is so middling, that the country would suffer very little by the entire destruction of its vineyards....

It appears by the indolent manner in which these works are conducted, that a fine field of discovery must remain to posterity.... But the court is so well satisfied with the discoveries now making, that it has forbid the earth to be dug any where else below a certain depth.

Johann Joachim Winckelmann
A Critical Account of the Situation and Destruction... of Herculaneum, Pompeii and Stabia, 1771

Herculaneum: an inventory

The Count de Caylus, archaeologist, writer and engraver (1692-1765), was fascinated by Pompeii and Herculaneum. Like Winckelmann, he resented the secrecy with which the Neapolitan court surrounded the site. He translated Winckelmann's pamphlet into French and made it more widely known, thereby exacerbating the suspicion with which the sovereigns regarded foreigners.

All the works of art found in Herculaneum are displayed in the exhibition rooms that his majesty the king of Sicily had built at Portici. Those entrusted with the protection of this collection, loyal to the instructions of their prince, will not allow a single note to be taken there, and nothing can escape their vigilance. The only remedy, therefore, is to remember at leisure the most important things you noticed, neglecting those details which even the best memory can retain only at the expense of more significant elements. This you may judge for yourselves by my brief account of the entire collection of antiquities to be found in the museum at Portici.

About 700 fragments of paintings; 350 statues, including portrait busts of varying quality, made of either bronze or marble; 700 different vases of various shapes and sizes, almost all of bronze and the majority designed for everyday use; about 20 bronze tripods; around 40 candelabras or chandeliers of the same metal, which supported the lamps used to light the apartments; 800 manuscripts; and 600 other smaller items, such as lamps, instruments, rings, bracelets, necklaces, mirrors, etc.

I include in the number of statues mentioned earlier all the small bronze and marble figurines which are nowadays to be found in almost every collection of antiquities. Such works deserve our attention only when they display elegant forms, when they reveal the attributes used to characterize the gods of the ancients, or, finally, when they provide a true likeness of those famous men whose actions and writings we so admire. I will confine myself to the mention of some small busts that bear the names of Epicurus, Zeno, Demosthenes and of the Epicurean philosopher Hermachus. The number of life-size statues amounts to about forty, of which approximately half are in bronze and the rest marble....

It would seem that at the time of the eruption of Vesuvius which destroyed the town of Herculaneum, the inhabitants had sufficient time to escape the danger and to rescue most of their belongings; this explains why no items of gold jewelry and only small silver vases have been found. Vases made of bronze have been unearthed in large quantities, and in general they reveal excellent workmanship and attractive forms. The decoration on these takes a hundred different forms, but is always tasteful. In some cases there are foliage motifs, inlaid with silver, encircling the rim or neck of the vase; in others pretty little intertwining figures form the handles; most take the form of jugs, bowls or saucers. Antique-dealers, who always try to elaborate on the history of the items they are selling in order to increase the value of their labours, will usually tell you that such vessels were sacrificial vases; but the vast quantities that are found every day in Herculaneum prove that they were simply made for everyday use. Nevertheless, the care taken to embellish them also shows, at the same time, that Greek influence was not confined to larger works, but extended even to the smaller objects. There is one such class of objects in particular that I cannot pass by without a mention: it consists of the different types of weighing scales, and especially those with two bronze feet, which are equivalent to about 11 inches of our imperial foot.

There is also a loaf that catches the attention of the curious; on it is an inscription, which would be difficult enough to read as it is, were one allowed to examine it without obstruction, and which is even more impossible to decipher since it has been covered with glass. The inscription consists of two lines, and I believe I could make out, in the second line, the Latin word for chick peas. It appears that the police ordered that every loaf be marked with the type

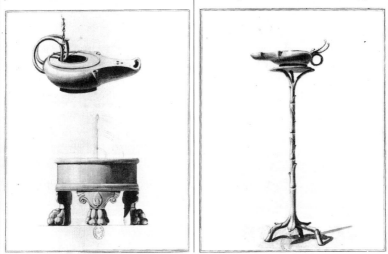

A Greek manuscript found in the Villa of the Papyri at Herculaneum.

of flour that had been used to make it.

As for the rest, all the different types of objects excavated in Herculaneum could provide material for several articles; but I only wish to deal here with the manuscripts, which seem to me the most significant finds. To get a clearer picture of these, you must imagine a fairly long strip of paper, about a foot wide. The whole length of this paper would have been covered with several columns of text, each separated from the next, and going from right to left. The sheet was then rolled up, in such a way, that as you opened the scroll, you had before you the first column or page of the work, the last one being at the centre of the roll.

The manuscripts from Herculaneum were found in a room in a palatial mansion, which has still not been fully excavated. They are made of Egyptian papyrus and are as black as coal. For a long while no one could think of a way of unrolling these papers, and, in their uncertainty, they decided to cut some of them in two lengthways, as if dividing a

of time, but which proved successful; and he has persisted with these experiments, at the same speed and with the same success. He looks for the outer edge of the manuscript and attaches to it several silk threads, which he rolls around some pins mounted on a small frame. He carefully turns these pins, and the manuscript unfolds almost imperceptibly. There is no hope of conserving the outer layers of paper, as these are always torn or rotten. You have to get down to a certain depth, when you reach the part of the manuscript that is only charred. Once a few columns have been unrolled, they are cut off and stuck onto a canvas support. It takes several months to unfold just one of these manuscripts, and in all the time since the work began, they have managed to save only the last thirty-eight columns of a Greek work condemning music. It is written by a certain Philodiorus, who is mentioned by Strabo and other ancient writers; his name and the subject of the book were fortunately discovered at the end of the manuscript. There are a few small gaps in the thirty-eight columns, but overall the writing is beautifully formed and clearly legible.

Two other columns from Greek manuscripts are on display; these were cut off before they discovered the secret of how to unroll them. Both seem to have been part of a philosophical treatise. The one I examined more carefully contains twenty-eight lines; I can remember twenty-three of them, which I shall constantly submit to the Académie. I also tried to memorize the shape of the letters and the number of them in each line of text, and I do not believe I have made any mistakes.

Count de Caylus

cylinder. This procedure allowed some of the writing to be seen quite clearly, but the manuscript as a whole was completely lost in the process. The numerous layers of papyrus were stuck together so tightly, that as they were detached, they were often reduced to dust. The most they could be hoped for using this method was to conserve a single page or column of a manuscript that might perhaps contain a hundred.

At this point a hard-working and patient monk introduced himself, and suggested a way of unrolling the manuscripts completely. He carried out experiments which took up a great deal

Italian journey

From the mid-18th century, artists and writers set out for Italy, hoping to discover there both the experience of a new country and memories of antiquity. Goethe, for example, from Germany, Stendhal and Hippolyte Taine from France, Dickens from England and Mark Twain from America brought back with them images, studies and impressions that shed light on our knowledge of the period as well as on their own personal sensibilities.

The painter Johann Heinrich Tischbein, who accompanied Goethe on his travels in Italy, left us this portrait of the great writer to commemorate their discovery of the ancient world.

Naples, Sunday 11 March 1787

As Tischbein and I drove to Pompeii, we saw on every hand many views which we knew well from drawings, but now they were all fitted together into one splendid landscape.

Pompeii surprises everyone by its compactness and its smallness of scale. The streets are narrow, though straight and provided with pavements, the houses small and windowless – their only light comes from their entrances and open arcades – and even the public buildings, the bench tomb at the town gate, the temple and a villa nearby look more like architectural models or dolls' houses than real buildings. But their rooms, passages and arcades are gaily painted. The walls have plain surfaces with richly detailed frescoes painted on them, most of which have now deteriorated. These frescoes are surrounded by amusing arabesques in admirable taste: from one, enchanting figures of children and nymphs evolve, in another, wild and tame animals emerge out of luxuriant floral wreaths. Though the city, first buried under a rain of ashes and stones and then looted by the excavators, is now completely destroyed, it still bears witness to an artistic instinct and a love of art shared by a whole people, which even the most ardent art lover today can neither feel nor understand and desire.

Considering the distance between Pompeii and Vesuvius, the volcanic debris which buried the city cannot have been driven here, either by the explosive force of the eruption or by a strong wind: my own conjecture is that the stones and ashes must have remained suspended in the air for some time, like clouds, before they descended upon the unfortunate city.

Naples, Sunday 18 March 1787

To picture more clearly what must have happened historically one should think of a mountain village buried in snow. The spaces between the buildings, and even the buildings themselves, crushed under the weight of the fallen material, were buried and invisible, with perhaps a wall sticking up here and there; sooner or later, people took this mound over and planted vineyards and gardens on it. It was probably peasants digging on their allotments who made the first important treasure hauls.

The mummified city left us with a curious, rather disagreeable impression, but our spirits began to recover as we sat in the pergola of a modest inn looking out over the sea, and ate a frugal meal. The blue sky and the glittering sea enchanted us, and we left hoping that, on some future day, when this little arbour was covered with vine leaves, we would meet there again and enjoy ourselves....

We could not put off any longer going to see Herculaneum and the Portici museum of objects excavated there. Herculaneum lay at the foot of Vesuvius and was completely buried under lava, to which subsequent eruptions added fresh layers, so that the ancient city is now sixty feet below ground level. It was discovered when, in the course of digging a well, some workmen came across floors of paved marble. It is a thousand pities that the site was not excavated methodically by German miners, instead of being casually ransacked as if by brigands, for many noble works of antiquity must have been thereby lost or ruined.

We descended a flight of sixty steps to a vault, where we admired by torchlight the former open-air theatre, while the guard told us about the things that were found there and brought to the light of day.

We had good letters of recommend-ation to the museum and were well received, but we were not allowed to make any drawings. Perhaps this made us pay attention even more closely to what we saw, so that we were all the more vividly transported into the past, when all these objects were part and parcel of their owners' daily life. They quite changed my picture of Pompeii. In my mind's eye its homes now looked both more cramped and more spacious – more cramped because I now saw them crowded with objects, and more spacious because these objects were not made merely for use but were decorated with such art and grace that they enlarged and refreshed the mind in a way that the physical space of even the largest room cannot do.

There was one beautiful jar, for example, with an exquisitely wrought rim which, on closer inspection, turned out to be two hinged semicircular handles, by which the vessel could be lifted and carried with ease. The lamps are decorated with as many masks and scrolls of foliage as they have wicks, so that each flame illuminates a different work of art. There were high, slender bronze pedestals, evidently intended as lamp stands. The lamps which were suspended from the ceiling were hung with all sorts of cunningly wrought figures which surprise and delight the eye as they swing and dangle.

We followed the custodians from room to room, trying to enjoy and learn as much as possible in the little time we had. We hope to come back.

Johann Wolfgang Goethe
Italian Journey, 1786-8

Naples, 5 April 1817

As I was leaving the *Museum of Antique Painting* at Portici, I met with a trio of English naval officers, who were on their way in. Now, this Museum contains no less than two-and-twenty rooms. On the road back into Naples, I kept up a steady gallop; yet before I reached the *ponte della Maddalena*, I was caught and overtaken by these same three English travellers, who, later in the evening, assured me that the paintings they had seen were positively *splendid,* and indeed one of the strangest sights in all the universe. The total time which they had spent inside the Museum amounted to somewhere between three and four minutes.

This collection, which affords such a treasure-house of curiosities for the true lover of art, consists of frescoes which have been removed from Pompeii and

Herculaneum. They reveal a complete absence of *chiaroscuro*, a very limited range of colour, a passable feeling for design and considerable facility. Two items in particular I found pleasing: *Orestes recognised by Iphigenia in ... Tauris,* and *Theseus thanked by the young Athenians for having delivered them from the Minotaur.* Both contain a wealth of noble simplicity, without a single theatrical gesture. The general impression is of a series of bad works by Domenichino, albeit further still removed from greatness by the presence of numerous faults of draughtsmanship – errors which this fine artist would never have committed. There are to be observed at Portici, among a host of minor, half-obliterated frescoes, five or six major productions on the scale of

Raphael's *Santa Cecilia.* Once upon a time, these frescoes served to ornament a bath-chamber at Herculaneum. Yet no one save a scholar could be so asinine as to claim that such stuff outweighs the *quattrocento*; in point of fact, it is nothing but a highly-remarkable artistic curio.

Stendhal
Rome, Naples and Florence, 1817

The Museo Borbonico

Most of the paintings of Pompeii and Herculaneum have been removed to the Museo at Naples. These consist principally of mural decorations, and generally without perspective, there being one or two figures on a dark background, with now and then animals, slight landscape views, and sections of architecture. The colouring is feeble, it being scarcely more than indicated, or rather subdued, effaced, and not by time (for I have seen quite fresh pictures), but designedly. To attract the eye was not an aim in these somewhat sombre apartments; they delighted in an attitude or form of the body, the mind being entertained with healthy and poetic images of physical activity. I have derived more pleasure from these paintings than from the most celebrated of the Renaissance epoch. There is more nature, more life in them.

The subjects have no particular interest, consisting ordinarily of a male or female figure nearly nude, raising an arm or a leg; Mars and Venus, Diana finding Endymion, Briseis conducted by Agamemnon, and the like, dancers, fauns, centaurs, a warrior bearing away a female, who, so carried, is so much at her ease! Nothing more is requisite, because

When he visited Italy Stendhal was more interested in contemporary customs than in antiquities, as we can tell from his comments on Pompeian painting.

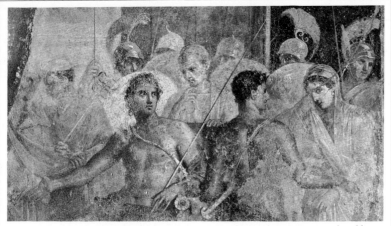

The subject of one of the frescoes described by Taine: Briseis, the young captive loved by Achilles, is carried off by Agamemnon.

you feel at once their beauty and repose. You cannot comprehend, before seeing it, how many charming attitudes a half-draped figure, floating in the air, can present to you; how many ways a veil can be raised, a flowing tunic arranged, a limb projected, and a breast exposed. The painters of these pictures enjoyed a unique advantage, one which no others have possessed, even those of the Renaissance, of living amidst congenial social customs, of constantly seeing figures naked and draped in the amphitheatre and in the baths, and besides this, of cultivating the corporeal endowments of strength and fleetness of foot. They alluded to fine breasts, well-set necks, and muscular arms as we of the present day do to expressive countenances and well-cut pantaloons.

Several days at Herculaneum and Pompeii

The first and most enduring is the image of the reddish-grey city, half ruined and deserted, a pile of stones on a hill of rocks, with rows of thick wall, and bluish flagging glittering in the dazzling white atmosphere; and surrounding this the sea, the mountains, and an infinite perspective.

On the summit stand the temples, that of Justice, of Venus, of Augustus, of Mercury, the house of Eumachia, and other temples, still incomplete, and, farther on, also on an elevation, the temple of Neptune. They also raised their gods on high in the pure atmosphere, of itself a divinity. The forum and the curia alongside afford a noble spot for councils, and to offer sacrifices. In the distance you discern the grand lines of the vapoury mountains, the tranquil tops of the Italian pine; then to the east, within the blonde sunlit haze, fine tree-forms and diversities of culture. You turn, and but little effort of the imagination enables you to reconstruct these temples. These columns, these Corinthian capitals, this simple arrangement, those openings of blue between those marble shafts, what an impression such a spectacle contemplated from infancy left on the mind! The city in those days was a veritable patrimony, and not, as now, a government collection of lodging-houses....

All these streets are narrow; the greater portion are mere lanes, over which one strides with ease. Generally there is room only for a cart, and ruts are still visible: from time to time wide stones afford a crossing like a bridge. These details indicate other customs than our own; there was evidently no great traffic as in our cities, nothing like our heavily-loaded vehicles, and fast-trotting fanciful carriages. Their carts transported grain, oil and provisions: much of the transportation was done on the arm and by slaves: the rich travelled about in litters. They possessed fewer and

Hippolyte Taine (1828-93) discovered Italy in the 1860s. As a historian, he aimed to place its men and monuments in their historical context.

different conveniences. One prominent trait of antique civilization is the absence of industrial pursuits. All supplies, utensils, and tissues, everything that machines and free labour now produce in such enormous quantities for everybody and at every price, were wanting to them. It was the slave who turned the mill-wheel: man devoted himself to the beautiful, and not to the useful; producing but little, he could consume but little. Life was necessarily simple.... A few thousands of proud, brave, temperate men..., who delighted in the view of a hill with a group of beautiful temples and statues, who entertained themselves with public business, and passed their days in the gymnasium, at the forum, in the baths and the theatre, who... were content with things as they stood; – such was the city of antiquity....

Almost everywhere in the centre of the house is a garden like a large saloon, and in the middle of this a marble basin, a fountain flowing into it, and the whole enclosed within a portico of columns. What could be more charming, and simple, and better disposed for the warm hours of the day? With green leaves visible between two white columns, red tiles against the blue of the sky, the murmuring water sparkling among flowers like a jet of liquid pearls, and those shadows of porticoes intersected by the powerful light; is there a more congenial place for the body to grow freely, for healthy meditation, and to enjoy, without ostentation or affectation, all that is most beautiful in nature and in life? Some of these fountains bear lions' heads, dogs, and fauns grouped around their margins. In the most capacious of all these houses, that of Diomed, orange and lemon trees, similar, probably, to those of ancient days, are putting forth their fresh green buds; a fishpool gleams

brightly, and a small colonnade encloses a summer dining-room, the whole embraced within the square of a grand portico. The more the imagination dwells on the social economy of antiquity, the more beautiful it seems, and the more conformable to the climate and the nature of man. The women had their *gynaeceum* in the rear behind the court and portico, a secluded retreat with no external communication, and entirely separated from public life. They were not very active in their small apartments; they indulged in indolent repose, like Italian ladies of the present day, or employed themselves on woollen fabrics, awaiting a father's or husband's return from the business and converse of men. Wandering eyes passed carelessly over obscure walls, dimly discerning, not pictures, as in our day, plastering them, not archaeological curiosities, and works of a different art and country; but figures repeating and beautifying ordinary attitudes, such as retiring to and arising from bed, the siesta, and various avocations; goddesses surrounding Paris, a Fortune, slender and elegant, like the females of Primaticcio, or a Deidamia frightened and falling backward on a chair. Habits, customs, occupations, dress, and monuments, all issue from one and a unique source; the human plant grew but on one stalk, which stalk had never been grafted....

The theatre crowns the summit of a hill; its seats are of Parian marble; in front is Vesuvius, and the sea radiant with morning splendour. Its roof was an awning, which, again, was sometimes wanting. Compare this with our nocturnal edifices, lighted by gas and filled with a mephitic atmosphere, where people pile themselves up in gaudy boxes ranged in rows like suspended cages; you then appreciate the difference between a gymnastic natural life with athletic forms, and our complicated artificial life with its dress-coats. The impression is the same in the majestic amphitheatre exposed to the sun, except that here is the blot of antique society, the Roman imprint of blood. The same impression you find in the baths; the red cornice of the *frigidarium* is full of charming airy little cupids, bounding away on horses or conducting chariots. Nothing is more agreeable and better understood than the drying room, with its vault covered with small figures in relief in rich medallions, and a file of Hercules ranged round the wall, their vigorous shoulders supporting the entablature. All these forms live and are healthy; none are exaggerated or overloaded. What a contrast on comparing with this our modern bathhouse, with its artificial, insipid nudities, its sentimental and voluptuous designs. The bathhouse nowadays is a washroom; in former times it was a pleasant retreat and a gymnastic institution. Several hours of the day were devoted to it: the muscles got to be supple and the skin brilliant; man here savoured of the voluptuous animality which permeated his alternately braced and mollified flesh; he lived not only through the head, as now, but through the body.

We descend and leave the city by the Street of Tombs. These tombs are almost entire; nothing can be nobler than their forms, nothing more solemn without being lugubrious. Death was not then surrounded with the torments of ascetic superstition, with ideas of hell; in the mind of the ancients it was one of the *offices* of man, simply a termination of life, a serious and not a terrible thing, which one regarded calmly and not with the shuddering doubts of Hamlet. The ashes and images of their ancestors were preserved in their dwellings; they saluted them on entering, and the living maintained intercourse with them; at the entrance of a city tombs were ranged on both sides of the street, and seemed to be the primitive, the original city of its founders. Hippias, in one of Plato's dialogues, says that 'that which is most beautiful for a man is to be rich, healthy, and honoured by Greeks, to attain old age, to pay funeral honours to his parents when they die, and himself to receive from his children a fitting and magnificent burial.'

The truest history would be that of the five or six ideas that rule in the mind of man – how an ordinary man, two thousand years ago, regarded death, fame, well-being, country, love, and happiness. Two ideas controlled ancient civilisation; the first, that of man, and the second, that of the city: to fashion a fine animal, agile, temperate, brave, hardy, and complete, and this through physical exercise and selection of good stock; and then to construct a small exclusive community, containing in its bosom all that man loved and respected, a kind of permanent camp with the exigences of continual danger; - these were the two ideas that gave birth to all the rest.

Hippolyte Taine
Travels in Italy, 1865

Charles Dickens spent nearly a year in Italy, in 1844-5, visiting Pompeii and Herculaneum and climbing Vesuvius towards the end of his tour. Pompeii's mixture of the macabre and the beautiful appealed strongly to his imagination, always fascinated by the thought of sudden death.

Stand at the bottom of the great market-place of Pompeii, and look up the silent streets, through the ruined temples of Jupiter and Isis, over the broken houses with their inmost sanctuaries open to the day, away to Mount Vesuvius, bright and snowy in the peaceful distance; and lose all count of time, and heed of other things, in the strange and melancholy sensation of seeing the Destroyed and the Destroyer making this quiet picture in the sun. Then, ramble on, and see, at every turn, the little familiar tokens of human habitation and every-day pursuits; the chafing of the bucket-rope in the stone rim of the exhausted well; the track of carriage-wheels in the pavement of the street; the marks of drinking-vessels on the stone counter of the wine-shop; the amphorae in private cellars, stored away so many hundred years ago, and undisturbed to this hour – all rendering the solitude and deadly lonesomeness of the place, ten thousand times more solemn, than if the volcano, in its fury, had swept the city from the earth, and sunk it in the bottom of the sea.

After it was shaken by the earthquake which preceded the eruption, workmen were employed in shaping out, in stone, new ornaments for temples and other buildings that had suffered. Here lies their work, outside the city gate, as if they would return to-morrow.

In the cellar of Diomede's house, where certain skeletons were found huddled together, close to the door, the impression of their bodies on the ashes, hardened with the ashes, and became stamped and fixed there, after they had shrunk, inside, to scanty bones. So, in the theatre of Herculaneum, a comic mask, floating on the stream when it was hot and liquid, stamped its mimic features in it as it hardened into stone; and now, it turns upon the stranger the fantastic look it turned upon the audiences in that same theatre two thousand years ago.

Next to the wonder of going up and down the streets, and in and out of the houses, and traversing the secret chambers of the temples of a religion that has vanished from the earth, and finding so many fresh traces of remote antiquity: as if the course of Time had been stopped after this desolation, and there had been no nights and days, months, years, and centuries, since: nothing is more impressive and terrible than the many evidences of the searching nature of the ashes, as bespeaking their irresistible power, and the impossibility of escaping them. In the wine-cellars, they forced their way into the earthen vessels: displacing the wine and choking them, to the brim, with dust. In the tombs, they forced the ashes of the dead from the funeral urns, and rained new ruin even into them. The mouths, and eyes, and skulls of all the skeletons, were stuffed with this terrible hail. In Herculaneum, where the flood was of a different and a heavier kind, it rolled in, like a sea. Imagine a deluge of water turned to marble, at its height – and that is what is called 'the lava' here.

Many of the paintings on the walls in the roofless chambers of both cities, or carefully removed to the museum at Naples, are as fresh and plain, as if they had been executed yesterday. Here are subjects of still life, as provisions, dead game, bottles, glasses, and the like; familiar classical stories, or mythological fables, always forcibly and plainly told; conceits of cupids, quarrelling, sporting, working at trades; theatrical rehearsals; poets reading their productions to their friends; inscriptions chalked upon the walls; political squibs, advertisements, rough drawings by schoolboys; everything to people and restore the ancient cities, in the fancy of their wondering visitor. Furniture, too, you see, of every kind – lamps, tables, couches; vessels for eating, drinking, and cooking; workmen's tools, surgical instruments, tickets for the theatre, pieces of money, personal ornaments, bunches of keys found clenched in the grasp of skeletons, helmets of guards and warriors; little household bells, yet musical with their old domestic tones.

The least among these objects, lends its aid to swell the interest of Vesuvius, and invest it with a perfect fascination. The looking, from either ruined city, into the neighbouring grounds overgrown with beautiful vines and luxuriant trees; and remembering that house upon house, temple on temple, building after building, and street after street, are still lying underneath the roots of all the quiet cultivation, waiting to be turned up to the light of day; is something so wonderful, so full of mystery, so captivating to the imagination, that one would think it would be paramount, and yield to nothing else. To nothing but Vesuvius; but the mountain is the genius of the scene. From every indication of the ruin it has worked, we look, again, with an absorbing interest to where its smoke is rising up into the sky. It is beyond us, as we thread the ruined streets; above us, as we stand upon the ruined walls; we

follow it through every vista of broken columns, as we wander through the empty court-yards of the houses; and through the garlandings and interlacings of every wanton vine. Turning away to Paestum yonder, to see the awful structures built, the least aged of them, hundreds of years before the birth of Christ, and standing yet, erect in lonely majesty, upon the wild, malaria-blighted plain – we watch Vesuvius as it disappears from the prospect, and watch for it again, on our return, with the same thrill of interest: as the doom and destiny of all this beautiful country, biding its terrible time.

Charles Dickens
Pictures from Italy, 1845

Mark Twain, who worked as a journalist before becoming a novelist, joined a group of American tourists on board 'Quaker City', the first cruise liner, for a tour of the Mediterranean. After visiting the Holy Land and Egypt, he and his travelling companions found themselves in Pompeii.

They pronounce it Pom-*pay*-e. I always had an idea that you went down into Pompeii with torches, by the way of damp, dark stairways, just as you do in silver mines, and traversed gloomy tunnels with lava overhead and something on either hand like dilapidated prisons gouged out of the solid earth, that faintly resembled houses. But you do nothing of the kind. Fully one-half of the buried city, perhaps, is completely exhumed and thrown open freely to the light of day; and there stand the long rows of solidly-built brick houses (roofless) just as they stood eighteen hundred years ago, hot with the flaming sun; and there lie their floors, clean-swept, and not a bright fragment tarnished or wanting of the labored mosaics that pictured them with the beasts, and birds, and flowers which we copy in perishable carpets to-day; and there are the Venuses, and Bacchuses, and Adonises, making love and getting drunk in many-hued frescoes on the walls of saloon and bed-chamber; and there are the narrow streets and narrower sidewalks, paved with flags of good hard lava, the one deeply rutted with the chariot-wheels, and the other with the passing feet of the Pompeiians of by-gone centuries; and there are the bake-shops, the temples, the halls of justice, the baths, the theatres – all clean-scraped and neat, and suggesting nothing of the nature of a silver mine away down in the bowels of the earth. The broken pillars

lying about, the doorless doorways and the crumbled tops of the wilderness of walls, were wonderfully suggestive of the "burnt district" in one of our cities, and if there had been any charred timbers, shattered windows, heaps of debris, and general blackness and smokiness about the place, the resemblance would have been perfect. But no – the sun shines as brightly down on old Pompeii to-day as it did when Christ was born in Bethlehem, and its streets are cleaner a hundred times than ever Pompeiian saw them in her prime. I know whereof I speak – for in the great, chief thoroughfares (Merchant street and the Street of Fortune) have I not seen with my own eyes how for two hundred years at least the pavements were not repaired! – how ruts five and even ten inches deep were worn into the thick flagstones by the chariot-wheels of generations of swindled tax-payers? And do I not know by these signs that Street Commissioners of Pompeii never attended to their business, and that if they never mended the pavements they never cleaned them? And, besides, is it not the inborn nature of Street Commissioners to avoid their duty whenever they get a chance? I wish I knew the name of the last one that held office in Pompeii so that I could give him a blast. I speak with feeling on this subject, because I caught my foot in one of those ruts, and the sadness that came over me when I saw the first poor skeleton, with ashes and lava sticking to it, was tempered by the reflection that may be that party was the Street Commissioner....

Then we lounged through many and many a sumptuous private mansion which we could not have entered without a formal invitation in incomprehensible Latin, in the olden time, when the owners lived there – and we probably wouldn't have got it. These people built their houses a good deal alike. The floors were laid in fanciful figures wrought in mosaics of many-colored marbles. At the threshold your eyes fall upon a Latin sentence of welcome, sometimes, or a picture of a dog, with the legend "Beware of the Dog", and sometimes a picture of a bear or a faun with no inscription at all. Then you enter a sort of vestibule, where they used to keep the hat-rack, I suppose; next a room with a large marble basin in the midst and the pipes of a fountain; on either side are bedrooms; beyond the fountain is a reception-room, then a little garden, dining-room, and so forth and so on. The floors were all mosaic, the walls were stuccoed, or frescoed, or ornamented with bas-reliefs, and here and there were statues, large and small, and little fish-pools, and cascades of sparkling water that sprang from secret places in the colonnade of handsome pillars that surrounded the court, and kept the flower-beds fresh and the air cool....

It was a quaint and curious pastime, wandering through this old silent city of the dead – lounging through utterly deserted streets where thousands and thousands of human beings once bought and sold, and walked and rode, and made the place resound with the noise and confusion of traffic and pleasure. They were not lazy. They hurried in those days. We had evidence of that. There was a temple on one corner, and it was a shorter cut to go between the columns of that temple from one street to the other than to go around – and behold that pathway had been worn deep into the heavy flag-stone floor of the building by generations of time-saving feet! They would not go around when it was quicker to go through. We do that way in our cities.

Every where, you see things that make you wonder how old these old houses were before the night of destruction came – things, too, which bring back those long dead inhabitants and place them living before your eyes. For instance: The steps (two feet thick – lava blocks) that lead up out of the school, and the same kind of steps that lead up into the dress circle of the principal theatre, are almost worn through! For ages the boys hurried out of that school, and for ages their parents hurried into that theatre, and the nervous feet that have been dust and ashes for eighteen centuries have left their record for us to read to-day....

And so I turned away and went through shop after shop and store after store, far down the long street of the merchants, and called for the wares of Rome and the East, but the tradesmen were gone, the marts were silent, and

"At the threshold your eyes fall upon a Latin sentence...: 'Beware of the Dog'.**"**

nothing was left but the broken jars all set in cement of cinders and ashes....

In a bake-shop was a mill for grinding the grain, and the furnaces for baking the bread: and they say that here, in the same furnaces, the exhumers of Pompeii found nice, well baked loaves which the baker had not found time to remove from the ovens the last time he left his shop, because circumstances compelled him to leave in such a hurry.

In one house (the only building in Pompeii which no woman is now allowed to enter) were the small rooms and short beds of solid masonry, just as they were in the old times, and on the walls were pictures which looked almost as fresh as if they were painted yesterday, but which no pen could have the hardihood to describe; and here and there were Latin inscriptions – obscene scintillations of wit, scratched by hands that possibly were uplifted to Heaven for succor in the midst of a driving storm of fire before the night was done.

In one of the principal streets was a ponderous stone tank, and a water-spout that supplied it, and where the tired, heated toilers from the Campagna used to rest their right hands when they bent over to put their lips to the spout, the thick stone was worn down to a broad groove an inch or two deep. Think of the countless thousands of hands that had pressed that spot in the ages that are gone, to so reduce a stone that is as hard as iron!

They had a great public bulletin board in Pompeii – a place where announcements for gladiatorial combats, elections, and such things, were posted – not on perishable paper, but carved in enduring stone. One lady, who, I take it, was rich and well brought up, advertised a dwelling or so to rent, with baths and all the modern improvements, and several hundred shops, stipulating that the dwellings should not be put to immoral purposes....

In one of these long Pompeiian halls the skeleton of a man was found, with ten pieces of gold in one hand and a large key in the other. He had seized his money and started toward the door, but the fiery tempest caught him at the very threshold, and he sank down and died. One more minute of precious time would have saved him. I saw the skeletons of a man, a woman, and two young girls. The woman had her hands spread wide apart, as if in mortal terror, and I imagined I could still trace upon her shapeless face something of the expression of wild despair that distorted it when the heavens rained fire in these streets, so many ages ago. The girls and the man lay with their faces upon their arms, as if they had tried to shield them from the enveloping cinders. In one

---

The tourists, eager for excitement, climbed Vesuvius after visiting the city destroyed by the terrible volcano.

apartment eighteen skeletons were found, all in sitting postures, and blackened places on the walls still mark their shapes and show their attitudes, like shadows. One of them, a woman, still wore upon her skeleton throat a necklace, with her name engraved upon it – JULIE DI DIOMEDE.

But perhaps the most poetical thing Pompeii has yielded to modern research, was that grand figure of a Roman soldier, clad in complete armor; who, true to his duty, true to his proud name of a soldier of Rome, and full of the stern courage which had given to that name its glory, stood to his post by the city gate, erect and unflinching, till the hell that raged around him *burned out* the dauntless spirit it could not conquer....

We came out from under the solemn mysteries of this city of the Venerable Past – this city which perished, with all its old ways and its quaint old fashions about it, remote centuries ago, when the Disciples were preaching the new religion, which is as old as the hills to us now – and went dreaming among the trees that grow over acres and acres of its still buried streets and squares, till a shrill whistle and the cry of '*All aboard – last train for Naples!*' woke me up and reminded me that I belonged in the nineteenth century, and was not a dusty mummy, caked with ashes and cinders, eighteen hundred years old. The transition was startling. The idea of a railroad train actually running to old dead Pompeii, and whistling irreverently, and calling for passengers in the most bustling and business-like way, was as strange a thing as one could imagine, and as unpoetical and disagreeable as it was strange.

Mark Twain
The Innocents Abroad, 1875

The Last Days of Pompeii

In Bulwer-Lytton's dramatic reconstruction of the final moments of Pompeii, the central characters, the lovers Glaucus and Ione, flee as a burning cloud of ash descends upon the city.

The progress of the destruction

The cloud, which had scattered so deep a murkiness over the day, had now settled into a solid and impenetrable mass. It resembled less even the thickest gloom of a night in the open air than the close and blind darkness of some narrow room. But in proportion as the blackness gathered, did the lightnings around Vesuvius increase in their vivid and scorching glare. Nor was their horrible beauty confined to the usual hues of fire; no rainbow ever rivalled their varying and prodigal dyes. Now brightly blue as the most azure depth of a southern sky – now of a livid and snakelike green, darting restlessly to and fro as the folds of an enormous serpent – now of a lurid and intolerable crimson, gushing forth through the columns of smoke, far and wide, and lighting up the whole city from arch to arch, – then suddenly dying into a sickly paleness, like the ghost of their own life!

In the pauses of the showers, you heard the rumbling of the earth beneath, and the groaning waves of the tortured sea; or, lower still, and audible but to the watch of intensest fear, the grinding and hissing murmur of the escaping gases through the chasms of the distant mountain. Sometimes the cloud appeared to break from its solid mass, and, by the lightning, to assume quaint and vast mimicries of human or of monster shapes, striding across the gloom, hurtling one upon the other, and vanishing swiftly into the turbulent abyss of shade; so that, to the eyes and fancies of the affrighted wanderers, the unsubstantial vapours were as the bodily forms of gigantic foes, – the agents of terror and of death.

The ashes in many places were already knee-deep; and the boiling showers which came from the steaming breath of the volcano forced their way into the houses, bearing with them a strong and suffocating vapour. In some places, immense fragments of rock, hurled upon the house roofs, bore down along the streets masses of confused ruin, which yet more and more, with every hour, obstructed the way; and, as the day advanced, the motion of the earth was more sensibly felt – the footing seemed to slide and creep – nor could chariot or litter be kept steady, even on the most level ground.

Sometimes the huger stones striking against each other as they fell, broke into countless fragments, emitting sparks of fire, which caught whatever was combustible within their reach; and along the plains beyond the city the darkness was now terribly relieved; for several houses, and even vineyards, had been set on flames; and at various intervals the fires rose suddenly and fiercely against the solid gloom. To add to this partial relief of the darkness, the citizens had, here and there, in the more public places, such as the porticos of temples and the entrances to the forum, endeavoured to place rows of torches; but these rarely continued long; the showers and the winds extinguished them, and the sudden darkness into which their sudden birth was converted had something in it doubly terrible and doubly impressing on the impotence of human hopes, the lesson of despair.

Frequently, by the momentary light of these torches, parties of fugitives encountered each other, some hurrying towards the sea, others flying from the sea back to the land, for the ocean had retreated rapidly from the shore – an utter darkness lay over it, and upon its groaning and tossing waves the storm of cinders and rock fell without the protection which the streets and roofs afforded to the land. Wild – haggard – ghastly with supernatural fears, these groups encountered each other, but without the leisure to speak, to consult, to advise; for the showers fell now frequently, though not continuously, extinguishing the lights, which showed to each band the deathlike faces of the other, and hurrying all to seek refuge beneath the nearest shelter. The whole elements of civilization were broken up. Ever and anon, by the flickering lights, you saw the thief hastening by the most . solemn authorities of the law, laden with, and fearfully chuckling over, the produce of his sudden gains. If, in the darkness, wife was separated from husband, or parent from child, vain was the hope of reunion. Each hurried blindly and confusedly on. Nothing in all the various and complicated machinery of social life was left save the primal law of self-preservation!

Through this awful scene did the Athenian wade his way, accompanied by Ione and the blind girl. Suddenly, a rush of hundreds, in their path to the sea, swept by them. Nydia was torn from the side of Glaucus, who, with Ione, was borne rapidly onward; and when the crowd (whose forms they saw not, so thick was the gloom) were gone, Nydia was still separated from their side. Glaucus shouted her name. No answer came. They retraced their steps – in vain: they could not discover her – it was evident that she had been swept along some opposite direction by the human current. Their friend, their preserver, was lost! And hitherto Nydia had been their guide. *Her blindness rendered the scene familiar to her alone.* Accustomed, through a perpetual night, to thread the windings of the city, she had led them unerringly towards the sea-shore, by which they had resolved to hazard an escape. Now, which way could they wend? all was rayless to them – a maze without a clue. Wearied, despondent, bewildered, they, however, passed along, the ashes falling upon their heads, the fragmentary stones dashing up in sparkles before their feet.

'Alas! alas!' murmured Ione, 'I can go no farther, my steps sink among the scorching cinders. Fly, dearest! – beloved, fly! and leave me to my fate!'

'Hush, my betrothed! my bride! Death with thee is sweeter than life without thee! Yet, whither – oh! whither, can we direct ourselves through the gloom? Already it seems that we have made but a circle, and are in the very spot which we quitted an hour ago.'

'O gods! yon rock – see, it hath riven the roof before us! It is death to move through the streets!'

'Blessed lightning! See, Ione – see! the portico of the Temple of Fortune is before us. Let us creep beneath it; it will protect us from the showers.'

He caught his beloved in his arms, and with difficulty and labour gained the temple. He bore her to the remoter and more sheltered part of the portico, and leaned over her, that he might shield her, with his own form, from the lightning and the showers! The beauty and the unselfishness of love could hallow even that dismal time!

'Who is there?' said the trembling and hollow voice of one who had preceded them in their place of refuge. 'Yet, what matters? – the crush of the ruined world forbids to us friends or foes.'

Ione turned at the sound of the voice, and, with a faint shriek, cowered again beneath the arms of Glaucus: and he, looking in the direction of the voice, beheld the cause of her alarm. Through the darkness glared forth two burning eyes – the lightning flashed and lingered athwart the temple – and Glaucus, with a shudder, perceived the lion to which he had been doomed couched beneath the pillars; – and, close beside it, unwitting of the vicinity, lay the giant form of him who had accosted them – the wounded gladiator, Niger.

That lightning had revealed to each other the form of beast and man; yet the instinct of both was quelled. Nay, the lion crept nearer and nearer to the gladiator, as for companionship; and the gladiator did not recede or tremble. The revolution of Nature had dissolved her lighter terrors as well as her wonted ties.

While they were thus terribly protected, a group of men and women, bearing torches, passed by the temple. They were of the congregation of the Nazarenes; and a sublime and unearthly emotion had not, indeed, quelled their awe, but it had robbed awe of fear. They had long believed, according to the error of the early Christians, that the Last Day was at hand; they imagined now that the Day had come.

'Woe! woe!' cried, in a shrill and piercing voice, the elder at their head. 'Behold! the Lord descendeth to judgment! He maketh fire come down from heaven in the sight of men! Woe! woe! ye strong and mighty! Woe to ye of the fasces and the purple! Woe to the idolater and the worshipper of the beast! Woe to ye who pour forth the blood of saints, and gloat over the death-pangs of the sons of God! Woe to the harlot of the sea! – woe! woe!'

And with a loud and deep chorus, the troop chanted forth along the wild horrors of the air, – 'Woe to the harlot of the sea! – woe! woe!'

The Nazarenes paced slowly on, their torches still flickering in the storm, their voices still raised in menace and solemn

"Frequently, by the momentary light of these torches, parties of fugitives encountered each other, some hurrying towards the sea, others flying from the sea back to the land."

warning, till, lost amid the windings in the streets, the darkness of the atmosphere and the silence of death again fell over the scene.

There was one of the frequent pauses in the showers, and Glaucus encouraged Ione once more to proceed. Just as they stood, hesitating, on the last step of the portico, an old man, with a bag in his right hand and leaning upon a youth, tottered by. The youth bore a torch. Glaucus recognised the two as father and son – miser and prodigal.

'Father,' said the youth, 'if you cannot move more swiftly, I must leave you, or we *both* perish!'

'Fly, boy, then, and leave thy sire!'

'But I cannot fly to starve; give me thy bag of gold!' And the youth snatched at it.

'Wretch! wouldst thou rob thy father?'

'Ay! who can tell the tale in this hour? Miser, perish!'

The boy struck the old man to the ground, plucked the bag from his relaxing hand, and fled onward with a shrill yell.

'Ye gods!' cried Glaucus: 'are ye blind, then, even in the dark? Such crimes may well confound the guiltless with the guilty in one common ruin. Ione, on! – on!'...

Advancing, as men grope for escape in a dungeon, Ione and her lover continued their uncertain way. At moments when the volcanic lightnings lingered over the streets, they were enabled, by that awful light, to steer and guide their progress: yet, little did the view it presented to them cheer or encourage their path....clear and distinct through all were the mighty and various sounds from the Fatal Mountain; its rushing winds; its whirling torrents; and, from time to time, the burst and roar of some more fiery and fierce explosion.

Edward Bulwer-Lytton
The Last Days of Pompeii, 1834

A Pompeian fantasy

The main character in Wilhelm Jensen's novella 'Gradiva' is an archaeologist called Dr Norbert Hanold. Standing in front of a bas-relief carving which shows a young girl, Gradiva, walking, the doctor falls into a deep, dreamlike state. Freud gave an interpretation of the novella, reading the whole thing as if it were the account of a patient; like every archaeologist, Freud believed, Hanold dreamed he was witnessing the catastrophic events at first hand.

In his dream, Dr Hanold finds himself face to face with Gradiva, in Pompeii, on 24 August 79. He then realizes that this young girl is none other than a childhood friend to whom he had never paid much attention. Her name is Zoë Bertgang, Zoë meaning 'life'.

All at once he felt certain that his return there today was futile. He would not find the girl he was hoping to meet, because she would not be allowed to come back until he himself was long dead, buried and forgotten, cut off from the land of the living. But as he walked along beside the wall on which the Judgment of Paris was painted, he suddenly caught a glimpse of Gradiva, right in front of him, looking exactly as she had the day before, wearing the same clothes, and sitting on the same step between the same two yellow columns. He refused to allow himself to be deceived by this product of his imagination, feeling sure that it was only his mind recreating before his very eyes a hallucination of what he had seen there the day before. Even so, he could not help gazing at the insubstantial vision that he had conjured up. He stood rooted to the spot, and almost before he realized he was speaking, there fell from his lips, in an agonized tone, the words: 'Oh! if only you were still alive, still existed!'

He fell silent, and there was not even a breath of wind to disturb the hush that once more descended on the ruins of the old hall. Until all at once another voice broke the empty stillness, saying: 'Wouldn't you prefer to sit down? You look tired.'

Norbert Hanold's heart missed a beat. He gathered together in his head as much sense as he could muster: a vision was incapable of speech. Or were his ears also playing tricks on him? He stared at her, leaning his hand on a column to steady himself.

The voice again asked him a question, and that voice could only be Gradiva's: 'Have you brought the white flower for me?'

He was gripped by a feeling of dizziness; realizing that he would have to sit down, as his legs could no longer support him, he allowed himself to slide down onto a step, until he was sitting opposite her, leaning against a column. She stared at him with her clear gaze, but the look in her eyes was quite different from the one she had given him the day before, when she had suddenly got up and left him. All trace of denial and displeasure had disappeared from her expression, as if she had since changed her opinion of him, and in their place was a searching curiosity and a desire to find out more....As he had still not answered her question, however, she spoke again, and said: 'Yesterday you told me that you had once called out to me as I was lying down to go to sleep, and that you had afterwards remained standing next to me; my face turned as white as marble, you said. When and where did this happen? I cannot remember such an incident, and I beg you to explain what happened in more detail.'

Norbert had by now regained sufficient control over his speech to be able to answer: 'It was night; you sat down on the steps of the Temple of Apollo in the Forum and the falling ashes from Vesuvius began to cover you.'

'Ah! – so that's when it was. Yes, that is true – I had forgotten. But I should have realized it would be something of that kind. When you mentioned it yesterday, it was all so unexpected; I was startled. But, if I am not mistaken, that happened almost two thousand years

ago. Were you alive then? You don't look that old to me.'

She spoke quite seriously; only towards the end of this speech did a slight, infinitely gentle smile play around the corners of her mouth. Norbert felt embarrassed and uncertain, and stuttered a little as he replied: 'No, I think in fact I had not yet been born at that point, in AD 79 – perhaps it was – yes, it must have been the state of mind that people call dreaming which carried me back to the time of the destruction of Pompeii. But I recognized you at first sight....'

A look of astonishment passed over the face of the young woman, who was sitting only a few steps away from him, and she repeated in a tone of wonder: 'You recognized me? In your dream? How?

'Initially, by the way you walk.'

'You noticed that? Is there something special about my walk, then?

Her amazement had visibly increased still further. He answered: 'Yes – are you not conscious of it yourself? You walk with more grace than anyone I have ever seen, or at least, than anyone alive today. But I also recognized you staight away by everything else: your face and figure, your bearing and your clothes. Because everything exactly matches your bas-relief portrait in Rome.

'Ah! I see...', she replied once more in the same tone, 'with my bas-relief portrait in Rome. I hadn't thought of that. And to be quite honest, I still don't entirely follow – what does it look like? – and have you seen it there?'

He then told her how, many years before, he had been fascinated by this relief and had been overjoyed to get hold of a plaster cast of it, which had been hanging in his room in Germany ever since. He looked at it every day, and he had become convinced that the picture represented a young girl from Pompeii, walking along over the flagstones of a street in her native city. This had been confirmed by his dream, and he now knew that it was also this dream that had forced him to travel here and find out whether he could discover any trace of her. At noon on the previous day, as he was standing on the corner of the Via del Mercurio, she had suddenly walked by before his very eyes, looking exactly as she did in her picture. She had seemed about to go into the House of Apollo, but a little farther on she had crossed the road again and disappeared in front of the House of Meleager.

She nodded and said: 'Yes, I was intending to visit the House of Apollo, but then I came here instead.'

He continued: 'This made me think of the Greek poet Meleager, and I thought you might be one of his descendants, returning... to the house of your ancestor. But when I spoke to you in Greek, you didn't understand me.'

'So that was Greek, was it? No, I don't speak it, or I have forgotten it, at least. But when you came back today, I heard you say something that I did understand. You expressed the wish that someone might still be there and alive. Only I didn't know who you meant.'

He replied that, when he had first seen her, he was convinced that it was not really her, but a figment of his imagination, an illusion that showed her sitting at the same spot where he had met her the day before. She smiled at this and answered: 'It would seem you have good reason to protect yourself from your excessively active imagination, though I would not have suspected it from the conversations we have had together.' Then she broke off, and continued: 'What is it about my walk, that you mentioned earlier?'

Clearly, she had developed an intense interest that would not allow her to abandon this point. He began: 'Would you mind...?'

But all at once he paused, as he remembered anxiously that the day before, when he had asked her if she would lie down and sleep on the steps again, as she had done at the Temple of Apollo, she had abruptly stood up and walked away.... Now, though, she continued to gaze at him with a calm and untroubled expression of sympathy, and as he did not go on, she said: 'It was kind of you to have me in mind, when you wished that someone could still be alive. Because of that, I will gladly do whatever you ask me to.'

Norbert's fears were allayed by these words, and he replied: 'It would make me very happy if I could see you walk by me the way you do in that relief....'

Without replying, she eagerly stood up and walked a little way between the wall and the row of columns. Her light and flowing gait resembled precisely the one that had impressed itself so clearly on his mind, the sole of her foot being lifted off the ground almost vertically with each step. But as he watched, Norbert realized for the first time that she was wearing light, sand-coloured shoes of fine leather beneath her short dress, rather than sandals. When she returned and sat down again in silence, he began in spite of himself to speak of the fact that her shoes were not the same as the ones in the relief. At this, she replied: 'Time changes everything, and sandals are unsuited to modern times; I wear shoes because they provide better protection from the dust and rain. But why did you ask me to walk in front of you? Is there something special about my walk?'...

Norbert explained that it had something to do with the way in which,

completely lost to them – with one possible exception: a woman who had once seemed to him to walk in this way. Naturally, he had been unable to confirm this at the time, because of the crowds of people milling around her....

'What a pity!' she answered, 'for if you had been able to confirm it, the information would have been of great scientific significance, and if you had succeeded in establishing it then, you would not have had to make the long journey here. But who is it you are talking about? Who is this Gradiva?'

'It was the name I gave to your portrait, because I didn't know your real name – and I still don't.'

These last words were added rather tentatively, and she also hesitated a little before responding to his implied question: 'My name is Zoë.'

He exclaimed in a voice full of pain: 'The name suits you perfectly, but to me it has a ring of bitter irony, for Zoë means "life".'

'We must accept the inevitable,' she answered, 'and I long ago grew used to the idea of being dead. My time has come to an end for today. You brought the flower of death for me,... so let me take it.'

Rising to her feet, she stretched out her delicate hand, and he offered her the stem of asphodel, taking care not to touch her fingers. Accepting the flower-covered stem, she said: 'Thank you. In spring people give roses to those who are more fortunate; but it is right that you should give me the flower of forgetfulness....With this, she walked away and vanished at the corner of the portico, just as she had done the previous day, as if the earth had swallowed her up.

Wilhelm Jensen
Gradiva, 1903

when she took a step forward, the back foot was raised almost vertically off the ground; he added that he had spent several weeks, in the streets of his native town, trying to study the way modern women walked, but it appeared that this beautiful manner of moving had been

The 'regime' of Amedeo Maiuri

Only in recent times has the rigorous approach of modern archaeologists enabled the excavations, the restoration and protection of Pompeii to be organized on a scientific basis. During his long period of work at the site Maiuri gave the city its definitive appearance.

'His thirty-seven years in charge of the excavations at Pompeii, between 1924 and 1961, enabled Amedeo Maiuri to benefit from an exceptional period of continuity. This great scholar developed a scientific approach which perfected our knowledge of the buried city, by excavating the lower levels of the site to provide new and illuminating evidence of its historical development. He also had greater success than some of his predecessors in restoring houses that had been excavated at various times in the past.

From 1924 to 1941 he concentrated on the area around the Via dell'Abbondanza, his main aim being to uncover the *insulae* on either side of the road, in order to gain a view of the whole: *insulae* 7, 6, the street between 6 and 10, *insula* 10 (two-thirds of which is occupied by the House of Menander, I, 10, 4), and insula 8. Maiuri followed the Via dell'Abbondanza for 140 m, to the

point where it reached the amphitheatre, which he also excavated, together with the palaestra, where the young men of Pompeii took their exercise. At the same time as he was completing work on the Villa of the Mysteries, he organized the digging of a trench over 8 m wide around the whole of the outside of the city wall, which had been discovered by Murat as early as 1813-14. This was to allow him to study the structure of the walls and towers, and to restore Tower X.

Maiuri next turned his attention to the southern part of the city between the Via delle Scuole and the Triangular Forum, where the houses rise one behind the other up the slope of the hill. First, he determined to clear away all the volcanic debris that was stacked up against the hillside. And in this way, one of the most unusual features of Pompeii was restored: its characteristic appearance of a city constructed on many levels, with houses descending in terraces, commanding a

spectacular view out over the steep drop and along the flank of the hill.

But Maiuri was not content to pursue his exploration of the buried city as a coherent whole. He felt it was only by deepening the excavations at the most significant, and topographically most important points – the forums, temples, city walls and oldest houses – that they could hope to shed light on the period of the city's origins, which were still obscure. For several years he carried out a systematic investigation of the pre-Roman and pre-Samnite strata. The discovery of the pre-Samnite city wall, in particular, allowed him to confirm the Greek influence that prevailed in the city after the battle of Cumae (474-450 BC). He pieced together the history of the Doric temple on the Triangular Forum in the Greek and Samnite periods; and he also proved that the

Etruscan element of the population had participated in the life of the temple and the cult of Apollo during the period of Etruscan domination of Pompeii (525-474 BC). Excavations in the civil forum led to the discovery of a series of shops dating from the Paleo-Samnite era. These surrounded the open space of a square which covered the same surface area as the present forum, though it lay in a different direction and had no portico. The remains of earlier dwellings found under private houses, such as the House of the Surgeon (VI, 1, 9-10), led Maiuri to revise upwards the date of the so-called limestone atrium ground-plan, to the middle and late Samnite periods, indicating clearly that the Pompeian atrium-house marks the end, rather than the beginning of a long sequence of development in municipal domestic design. Architectural surveys and analyses enabled Maiuri to pinpoint those elements of the city that date from its reconstruction after the earthquake of 62.

Credit must also go to Maiuri for much of the pleasure experienced by tourists in Pompeii, in that he was responsible for restoring the roofs of the House of Menander (I, 10, 4), and the Villa of the Mysteries, without neglecting more modest dwellings such as the House of the Lovers (I, 7, 7) and the House of the Moralist (V, 1, 18). Nor did he neglect the restoration of public monuments, such as the tribunal of the basilica, the Tomb of the Istacidii, the row of columns around the Triangular Forum, as well as the exquisite monopteros around the sacred well there, built by the Samnite magistrate Numerius Trebius.

In September 1943 repeated bombardments added to the catalogue of disasters suffered by Pompeii since ancient times. Yet here, as elsewhere, the destruction often proved fruitful for archaeological science; beneath the Antiquarium was found a villa that had not been robbed by the earthquake of its impressive paintings in the *triclinium,* and outside the city walls, in the suburb of S. Abbondio, the crater left by a bomb led to the discovery of the first blocks of a temple of Dionysos dating from the pre-Roman and Roman periods.

In 1951 work on the site was at last resumed, thanks to new resources... with the idea that the volcanic rubble cleared from Pompeii might be used to enrich the soil of the surrounding countryside. Of the 66 ha that make up the walled city, at least 26 ha had yet to be excavated, not including the areas just outside the walls and the suburbs. The first task was to excavate Regions I and II, which are separated by the *cardo* that leads out to the Nucerian Gate: *insulae* I, 9 and II, 3 were brought to light, and so too was II, 4, occupied entirely by the House of Julia Felix, which had previously been uncovered in 1755-7, only to be reburied! *Insula* 5 was found to have been planted with a vineyard, and the Via dell'Abbondanza was followed to its end at the Sarnian Gate, a total of 1080 m from the forum.

More than 500,000 cubic metres of earth and centuries-old debris were removed from around the city wall between the Marine Gate and the Greek theatre, the Stabian Gate and the amphitheatre. And there now reappeared a view of the fine houses of Region VIII, whose large windows and terraces opened onto the panorama of the valley below, the mountains and the sea. The city wall was revealed to greater advantage, and above all the rich cemetery outside the Nucerian Gate provided a fresh harvest of inscriptions which shed light on the various classes of Pompeian society.

Over the last twenty years the excavations have continued under the guidance of A. de Franciscis, F. Zevi and, most recently, Mrs Irulli Cerulli: the House of Fabius Rufus has been uncovered in the *insula occidentalis,* to the west of Regions VI and VII, as well as that of C. Julius Polybius (IX, 13, 1-3). But worries as much as triumphs absorb the energies of the directors, as they attempt to conserve this highly prestigious site, which is visited by over a million people each year. Their main concern is to safeguard the Pompeian miracle, which, after many years of indifference, the Italian government has at last begun to treat with more sensitive awareness, since the introduction of special legislation in 1976.

Robert Etienne

Maiuri through the eyes of one of his contemporaries

In his book 'Travels in Italy' the Italian writer Guido Piovene created a vivid portrait of the famous archaeologist.

A little below average height, with one shoulder slightly lower than the other, Maiuri, this prince among archaeologists, seems to watch you out of the corner of his eye; obliquely, he envelops you in the

Maiuri in Pompeii, in raincoat and hat, 1955

the same impression of basic gentleness, this gracious air of good-natured bonhomie, this almost intangible yet seductive warmth, with which Naples herself welcomes strangers; and it leaves you with the impression of having had as your guide the winged spirit which in Shakespeare's comedies leads the people lost in the forest. Maiuri walks with small steps, but he walks for hours at a stretch, as seems to be taught in the great school of archaeology. An archaeologist is not just an office worker, but a lover of the open air. And he has the knack – which, I am sad to say, seems to be dying out – of not imposing on you the great weight of his erudition, but only saying what he knows will be of interest to his interlocutor. In sum, he is one of the great lords of this lordly city, happy to welcome visitors to the site of the excavations and to do the honours.

gaze of his bright eyes, which, though they can sometimes be hard and piercing, are almost always gentle, with an extraordinary mobility of expression. It is

Guido Piovene
Travels in Italy, 1958

The cost of living in Pompeii

The work of every archaeologist includes the collection of small indications and apparently insignificant objects that will allow the background to daily life to be meticulously reconstructed: for example, the scale of prices for various goods in the currency of the period.

Foodstuffs

one *modius* (6.503 kg) of corn	12 asses
one *modius* of wheat	30 asses
one *modius* of lupins	3 asses
a pound (0.328 kg;) of oil	4 asses
a measure of ordinary wine	1 as
a measure of Falernian wine	4 asses

Utensils

stewing pot	1 as
plate	1 as
small drinking vase	2 asses
bucket	9 asses
lamp	1 as
silver sieve	90 deniers

Clothing

tunic	15 sesterces
for washing a tunic	1 denier

Animals

mule	520 sesterces

1 sesterce = 4 asses
1 denier = 4 sesterces

Slaves	
two slaves	5048 sesterces

The fact that the cost of living in Pompeii was relatively low is confirmed by the account book for a household of three people, including a slave, which reveals the contents of the Pompeian woman's 'shopping basket' for the eight days before the Ides. The items are listed below:

8th day before the Ides

cheese		1 as
bread		8 asses
oil		3 asses
wine		3 asses
	Total	15 asses

7th day before the Ides

bread		8 asses
oil		5 asses
onions		5 asses
stewing pot		1 as
bread for slave		2 asses
wine		2 asses
	Total	23 asses

6th day before the Ides

bread		8 asses
bread for slave		4 asses
semolina		3 asses
	Total	15 asses

5th day before the Ides

wine for the *domator* (trainer)		16 asses
bread		8 asses
wine		2 asses
cheese		2 asses
	Total	28 asses

4th day before the Ides

hxeres (?)		16 asses
bread		2 asses
femininum (?)		8 asses
hard wheat		16 asses
bubella (?)		1 as
dates		1 as
incense		1 as
cheese		2 asses
black pudding		1 as
soft cheese		4 asses
oil		7 asses
	Total	59 asses

3rd day before the Ides

mountain *servato* (?)		17 asses
oil		25 asses
bread		4 asses
cheese		4 asses
leek		1 as
plate		1 as
bucket		9 asses
lamp		1 as
	Total	62 asses

2nd day before the Ides

bread		2 asses
bread for slave		2 asses
	Total	4 asses

Day before the Ides

bread for slave		2 asses
large loaf		2 asses
leek		1 as
	Total	5 asses

Ides

bread		2 asses
large loaf		2 asses
oil		5 asses
semolina		3 asses
for the *domator*, small fishes		2 asses
	Total	14 asses

The secret of the Villa of the Mysteries

The Villa of the Mysteries, a vast ninety-room mansion which was only discovered at the beginning of the 20th century, contains the most famous of all Pompeian frescoes. According to a recent study, by Gilles Sauron, it seems that the cycle should be read not as a continuous frieze, but symmetrically along each wall, the frieze on the right representing the main stages in the apotheosis of Semele, and that on the left, the apotheosis of Dionysos.

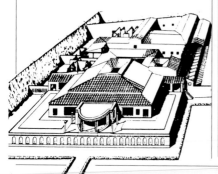

Two separate, but parallel series of images converge on the divine couple Dionysos and Semele (above left), guarantors of immortality. They illustrate the rites undergone by a lady of the Roman aristocracy as she is initiated into the Dionysiac cult.

The *domina* of the villa (below left), the priestess, is represented as a universal example. The most important moments of her life are placed in the context of successive episodes in the apotheosis of Semele and Dionysos.

The myth of Semele

Semele's union with Zeus and the marriage of the priestess. The scene shows preparations for a wedding, in the presence of two Eros figures; one offers a mirror, while the other contemplates the scene, bow in hand.

Semele's pregnancy and the first initiation rite. A maenad turns towards a woman carrying a *thyrsus*, a staff entwined with vine leaves and ivy, which symbolizes the child that is about to be born.

The annihilation of Semele and the second initiation rite. From right to left: the initiate kneels to take refuge in the lap of a seated woman, whose hair is arranged in the traditional manner for wet-nurses and midwives. A winged demon is about to strike the initiate with a whip, symbolizing the lightning that killed Semele, while a torchbearer prepares to reveal the hidden phallus, a gesture that may represent childbirth. The scene as a whole symbolizes the priestess's participation in the annihilation of Semele, and therefore in her apotheosis.

The myth of Dionysos

The education of Dionysos. A woman dressed in a *peplos* watches a young boy who is wearing nothing but a pair of high boots; he is reading, while a seated woman rests her right hand on his shoulder. In this image, the idea of study is related to that of initiation. The priestess is portrayed in her role as teacher, through both the figure of the secular mother and, in the context of the myth of Dionysos, that of the god's nurse.

The death of Dionysos and the priestess's role in the initiation of men into the Mysteries. Here, ritual actions are directly associated with the legend of the future god. A woman brings a plate piled with cakes; the priestess appears, crowned with an olive wreath, and lifts the corner of a veil that covers a basket. A servant pours a fine trickle of water onto the olive branch held out to her by her mistress. This no doubt refers to some funerary rite, the purpose of which is to prepare for the resurrection and apotheosis of Dionysos. The priestess is shown in her sacerdotal function, participating in the dramatic death of the god and in his implied resurrection.

The spreading of the Dionysiac cult and the priestess's initial fear before embracing the religion. Here we find the priestess, dressed as an elegant Greek citizen, in the centre of a composition that includes the same three people, first on her right, and then on her left. She is terrified, as we can see from her expression and from the gesture of her left hand; the cloak billowing out above her head is a conventional way of indicating attempted flight. On her right, a Silenus figure crowned with a laurel wreath plays his lyre and sings a funeral dirge in honour of the dead Dionysos; two shepherds with goats' ears accompany him. On the left, the same three figures are preparing to present a spectacle, probably a dance. The priestess is disturbed by the appearance of these representatives of an apparently barbarous and archaic religion. Yet while remembering the fears she experienced on the eve of her conversion, she shows that her misgivings were irrational and unfounded. For the god who finally appears at the centre of the composition is the god of eternal youth, who, even on Mount Olympus, finds comfort in his mother's lap.

Universal and beneficent, Dionysos, far from encouraging ignorance amongst his rustic cortege of Silenus characters, urges the initiates to study books; literature is an essential stage on the route that leads to him.

The Boscoreale Treasure

In 1895 a man working on the excavation of a large villa at Boscoreale, not far from Pompeii, discovered at the bottom of a wine vat a silver treasure, which a servant had no doubt hurriedly tried to protect at the time of the eruption. This complete set of Roman tableware can today be seen in the Louvre in Paris.

For a long time Roman society under the Republic refused, often with exaggerated scorn, to employ tableware made of precious metals; Pliny reports that the Carthaginian ambassadors received in Rome by senatorial families were astonished to find only two or three pieces from a single silver dinner service presented at every meal. The great treasures of the early Imperial period indicate the enormous changes brought about by the conquest of the East and the Carthaginian wars, which sent 'corrupting gold' flooding into Rome.

Silver plate remained a luxury for a considerable time, however; a single goblet often represented the only

A mirror, with a bust of Dionysos. Above right, a silver cup with raised decoration illustrates the triumphal procession of Tiberius.

investment of a person of modest means, a soldier or shopkeeper, who would jealously have his name inscribed upon it. A collection as large as that from Boscoreale, made up of 109 pieces in all, could only have belonged to rich landowners, and even they would not have been able to purchase the service all in one go. Some particularly valuable pieces, considered essentially as works of art, may have been obtained as part of an inheritance – the three *phiales* with relief decoration, for example; but other objects passed from hand to hand, as we can see from the names of three successive owners inscribed on the base of the vases decorated with olive branches.

Although it remained the preserve of the rich, silver plate had nevertheless spread into every sphere of daily life by the early 1st century AD, as we can judge from the fact that three elaborate mirrors, belonging to a lady's toilet, also formed part of the Treasure. The greater part of the collection is made up of items of tableware, drinking vessels, dishes and other accessories.

Boscoreale does not perhaps offer the same range of forms as the treasure found in the House of Menander – a veritable typological repertoire of 1st-century Roman tableware – but it does provide examples of the most important items, many of which are grouped in pairs; the weight markings on the reverse of the objects often refer to the combined weight of the two matching pieces in a pair, rather than to that of the individual item.

Written and visual documents, particularly paintings and mosaics, often provide information on how the various vessels were actually used. In spite of the richness of the decoration on some of the pieces, we should not forget that most of

them would have been used, if not on a daily basis, then at least for important banquets; a fine array of silver tableware would have been the pride of every host. 'Silverware, my very own silverware, is my great passion', proclaimed Trimalchio, Petronius' parvenu millionaire in the *Satyricon.*

The Treasure reveals great artistic and technical skill

Pergamum and Alexandria, the great centres of Hellenistic art, had attained a remarkably high standard of metalwork, and they had a direct influence on Rome, especially during the early years of the Empire. Not only objects, but also artists and craftsmen travelled from Greece to Italy, where they spread their techniques and repertoire of decorative motifs; the elaborate, yet elegant swirling foliage that decorates the lower portion of the wall around the *Ara Pacis* (Altar of Peace), erected in 13 BC to celebrate Augustus' return to Rome, was almost certainly inspired by Pergamanian silverware. Yet an almost identical pattern of plant stems curling symmetrically on either side of a vertical central stalk can be found on two of the drinking vases from Boscoreale; the composition is enlivened by the occasional animal appearing amid the leaves, or larger groups of creatures placed on large floral bouquets. They provide fine examples of how plant motifs could be interpreted in both a geometric and more imaginative fashion, without the original fluidity of the design being lost – a characteristic of the 'inhabited foliage' motif developed during the Hellenistic era.

The same taste in decoration can be found in another context on two pairs of drinking vessels, one decorated with olive-tree leaves, the other with plane-tree branches; in the former, the rounded forms of the olives in high repoussé relief contrast with the smooth, flat surfaces and sharp angles of the leaves in lower relief, while in the latter, the curving silhouettes of the plane tree leaves are delicately outlined.

The motifs are not original, as goblets decorated with olives also formed part of the treasure from the House of Menander, but a comparison indicates the superior artistic and technical quality of those from Boscoreale; the fluidity of the lines and the careful rendering of details reveal the exceptional quality and high artistic value of this metalwork.

The same qualities – skill in execution, sensitivity to the decorative motif, and a taste for nature – can also be found in the crane and stork goblets, a highly suitable subject borrowed from Hellenistic art, and more specifically from Nilotic subjects, but treated here as a sequence of moments observed from life and presented rather in the manner of a cartoon strip. The 'sufferings of a family of storks' show the parents struggling first with an undesirable host, then with a fellow scrounger, and finally with their starving offspring. Similarly, vases decorated with *xenia*, utensils and food prepared for a banquet, depict an extremely appetizing succession of sketches: a trussed piglet, a hare and a basket of fruits.

Every piece of silver plate is richly decorated

Petronius' vivid description of Trimalchio's feast provides us with abundant information about the richness and variety of the tableware that came to be used more and more widely, in the provincial cities as well as in Rome – a custom that even the Barbarians approved of.

In addition to plain containers, goblets, saucers and trays, Petronius describes at great length the sumptuous tablecloths and precious vases decorated with mythological scenes. The highlight of the freedman's spectacle is the appearance on the table of a jointed silver skeleton, which offers him the opportunity of making a pompous speech about the brevity of life; here, farcical Epicurean maxims are placed in the mouth of a glutton, but this was also in fact the traditional theme of all Roman banquets, as the two famous skeleton goblets indicate.

Four tableaux on each vessel introduce the skeletons of Greek poets and philosophers – Sophocles, Menander, Zeno and Epicurus, as well as other anonymous figures. The images are quite clear, but are supplemented by inscriptions, which point out who each one is, or draw out the moral of the scene; where one of the skeletons is weighing a heavy purse against a butterfly, symbol of the human soul, for example, the purse is labelled 'wisdom'. 'Enjoy life while ye may', comments one inscription; 'Life is a theatre', states another. Black humour, quite common in Pompeii, can be either vicious – 'Honour filth' is the sarcastic comment on the scene showing a skeleton offering

A silver goblet (10.4 cm high), one of the most beautiful pieces in the Boscoreale Treasure. Skeletons are grouped in four separate scenes, beneath garlands of roses.

a libation to his dead companion – or mocking: Epicurus seizes a huge portion of an enormous cake, under the disapproving eye of Zeno. The Greek thinkers provide a warning presence in this interpretation of Epicurus' often misunderstood philosophy.

Two goblets covered with Bacchic scenes bear witness to a completely different spirit. The origin of the motifs is the same, Hellenistic art, and these Dionysiac revels may remind us of the processions organized in Alexandria by Ptolemy VII, reviving memories of Bacchus' Indian triumph. Here, however, the motif appears in its most basic form, devoid of the religious significance that can be found, for instance, in certain paintings in Pompeii and, later, on sarcophagi. In this case it is the more picturesque and amusing aspects of the scene that have fired the silversmiths' imagination: the dainty putti, contrasted with the powerful lion and elephant – aspects of a Bacchic repertoire that frequently makes its appearance on drinking vessels in various guises, including masks, garlands and more elaborate scenes.

Outstanding pieces: the 'Cleopatra' *phiale*, a marine *thiasos* and *oenochoes*

The most impressive piece in the collection is without doubt the *phiale* decorated with an embossed head of Alexandria. It has been suggested that the young woman, who wears on her head the elephant skin that characterizes personifications of the Egyptian city, may be a portrait of Cleopatra VII. She is surrounded by a host of religious attributes evoking divinities of the Graeco-Roman and Egyptian pantheons, an indication of the fervent experimentation with all forms of religion that occurred in certain parts of

society towards the end of the Republic. This remarkably fine vessel, heightened by subtle gilding, is essentially a work of art which would probably have been displayed on a dresser for the admiration of guests, rather like the other two *phiales* in the Treasure, decorated with the repoussé portrait busts of an Augustan couple, and similar pieces in the Hildesheim Treasure.

Most of the objects from Boscoreale therefore derive their decoration from the familiar metalwork repertoire, and, in a more general way, from the minor Hellenistic arts. Certain motifs, however, adopted purely by Roman art, are direct borrowings from Greek prototypes: the Victories tearing the throats of their victims on a pair of *oenochoe,* for example, can be found in an identical form in Trajan's forum, and also on gold coins from Lampsacus (4th century BC).

Two exceptional items from the Treasure, held in a private collection, indicate the craftsmen's desire to employ this purely Roman repertoire. As early as the 3rd and 2nd centuries BC, painters and sculptors were fond of depicting contemporary events in the native Italic tradition, and Roman art often shows that it had no qualms about juxtaposing elements from the Greek tradition with those evolved in a quite different context, in Rome itself. At the beginning of the 1st century BC, for example, on the monument traditionally referred to as the Altar of Domitius Ahenobarbus, we find side by side a marine *thiasos* in the Scopas tradition and a historical relief, depicting scenes of census and sacrifice whose meaning is still in doubt. But what had until now been mere eclecticism, the arbitrary juxtaposition of two wholly different artistic traditions, was moulded under Augustus into a classical style, a perfect blend of the spirit of a past age

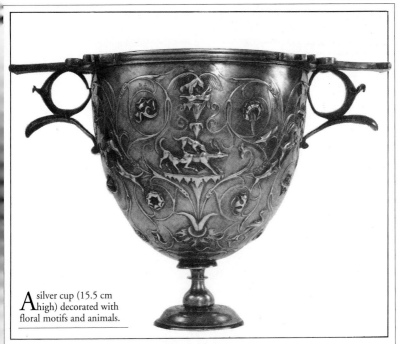

A silver cup (15.5 cm high) decorated with floral motifs and animals.

with that of the present. The *Ara Pacis*, discussed earlier, is the most striking product of this fusion in the realm of official art; the Boscoreale is the finest example in the minor arts. Indeed, two goblets bear on their sides historical scenes which show, on the one hand, Augustus (receiving the *clipeus virtutis* awarded to the emperor by the Senate?) and, on the other, Tiberius.

The silver treasure from Boscoreale therefore offers a clear indication of the refinement of the Roman aristocracy and bourgeoisie at the beginning of the Imperial period; from this time on, the development of a clientele capable of appreciating the products of the minor arts, combined with the move in taste towards increased luxury, resulted in a

remarkable expansion in the production of such objects. The Boscoreale Treasure, which represents both a high level of technical achievement and growing confidence in decorative taste, in the choice of motifs and in their execution, through its combinination of skill in the way the metal is worked and discreet application of gilding, bears witness both to the artistic ability of the metalworking ateliers and to the luxurious living conditions of the wealthy Campanian landowners.

François Baratte
Archeologia, no. 54, January 1973

The second death of Pompeii

What Vesuvius spared in AD 79, men are now in the process of destroying. The Italian government has blocked the 36 million lire earmarked by the European Community in 1984 for the restoration of Pompeii. Vegetation, damp, vandalism and hordes of tourists are finishing off the ghost town. It is an archaeological tragedy of the first order.

Pompeii, Easter 1979: there is a vast crowd of tourists. Amongst the buildings stands a private house not open to the public, where, in the atrium, or inner courtyard, the stone columns are still standing. It is impossible to keep an eye on everyone. Some of the tourists find their way into the courtyard and, by way of a game, start to push against the columns. Eventually they succeed in knocking them down. 'Fun' like this is apparently quite common. Indeed, it is reported that there are even competitions to see who can bring the columns down quickest. Give or take a month, it was then 1900 years since Vesuvius' destruction of the city. The two events are not without their parallels. Archaeologists who know Pompeii well have a great deal to say on the subject. For even since 1980, when an earthquake caused much damage to the famous site, Pompeii has been the scene of a permanent catastrophe. Year by year, day by day, the city is being destroyed – and largely because of man.

It must be used to it by now. Seventeen years before the disaster that buried it, the city was devastated by an earthquake. At the time of the eruption several buildings had just been rebuilt, while others were still being restored. The wool market, for example, had lost part of its rubble facade; this section had been replaced with brick, but the facing had yet to be applied to disguise the discordant mixture of materials – when suddenly, 24 August AD 79 dawned.

The city's second existence began with its gradual rediscovery in the 18th century

But just when Pompeii was being 'revived', according to the accepted phrase, it began to die its second death. Not only because the early excavations,

carried out over two hundred years ago and again in the 19th century, often turned out to be more of a massacre – what fun to carry off statues and fling around inscribed bronze plaques! – but also because all the remains preserved by the catastrophic eruption, were now exposed to the extremes of the weather, to vegetation, and to man.

Even before the most recent earthquake, the situation was not ideal. But Pompeii nevertheless retained its attractive appearance; photographers could still enjoy working there. The shocks of 23 November 1980 sent columns, whole walls or sections of wall and certain upper storeys crashing to the ground, and left several others leaning dangerously. Entire areas of the city were closed to visitors; props and struts were introduced. As elsewhere in Italy, the entrance fee was suddenly increased: from 150 to 4000 lire.

Save Pompeii: a cry across the world. But who listened to it?

In 1983 the authorities in charge of the site asked the French archaeologist Jean-Pierre Adam to prepare a technical report on the damage sustained by the city, to evaluate all possible methods of restoration and the various remedies that could be employed. In 1984 the European Community awarded the sum of 36 million lire for the restoration of Pompeii, the first payment to be made available from the beginning of 1985.

Was Pompeii about to be rescued? In 1985 a new superintendent was appointed. He promised to implement all the report's findings. Yet the result was a complete stoppage to all archaeological work on the site. Of course, archaeologists continued to travel from all over the world to see what was going on, in their own time and paying their own expenses. They returned dismayed. In spite of the efforts of their Italian colleagues, in spite of the huge increase in entrance tariffs and the considerable size of the available budget, in spite of the drastic reduction of the area open to the public, the situation was not improving; in fact, if anything, it was getting worse. The report has still not produced any results. No work has been commissioned, no contract has been signed with the excellent institutes of restoration that exist within Italy itself, in Florence and in Rome, and which are generally considered the best in the world. The 36 million lire are waiting, they say, for 'technical and administrative problems which have yet to be resolved'.

Pompeii suffers from pollution; the worst forms of damage are of human origin

Some damage is caused quite innocently. The site receives about half a million visitors a year; it has become the great public park of the Naples region, filled with buildings, and it welcomes an average 4500 tourists on each opening day. Almost 22,000 visitors have been counted on certain Easter Mondays. These visitors, inevitably, walk around, and in walking they wear down the roads. In particular, they wear down any pavements left in antiquity without a stone covering. Below the surface of these pavements run lead drains, ancient drains reconstructed after the earthquake of 62, and placed at that time – provisionally, so they thought – not far from the surface. Little by little the tourists erode the soil, until these lead pipes are uncovered; they tread on them; the lead is crushed, cracks, and eventually often disappears altogether.

The stone-covered pavements suffer too. Cracks open up in the mortar or in the mosaic of pebbles. Bit by bit, the covering, trampled and kicked, falls to pieces. Only the paving slabs of the streets themselves stand up to this harsh treatment, as these were always carved from solid lava and were designed to withstand the passage of the carts. The edges of the pavements, however, are often made of volcanic tufa or limestone, soft stones that are eroded by the constant wear and tear, worn down and deformed. This happened in Roman times, too, but then they would have been replaced. Visitors to Pompeii should surely be made to walk in the street, not on the pavements. In the

famous Via dell'Abbondanza the constant passage of feet has worn the pavements down to the same level as the road, and in some places even below it.

To this gradual, and usually accidental, type of damage can be added less innocent forms

Graffiti continue to multiply, the vandals preferring to leave their mark on the few paintings that are still in good condition. People pull gently at the edge of a layer of plaster that is starting to come away – and there are plenty of these. They get into the forbidden areas, by clambering over the barriers or by whatever other means they can find, and amuse themselves to the extent of committing acts of vandalism, pure and simple....

Another favourite pastime is to pick up remains, to carry off small pieces of stucco or pottery, or fragments of marble. Paintings are particularly popular. Not to be carried away in one piece to be offered for sale later – that would be too difficult. Instead, the best part – a decorative motif, a human figure, an animal, a small tableau – is roughly hacked out. This kind of activity is not a recent development, of course; it represents the continuation of an age-old practice. Traditions die hard in Campania, whether they are encouraged by tourists or faithfully maintained by the inhabitants of the region.

In reading books on Pompeii, people are often surprised by the small number of minor objects found there – statuettes, for example – even on the site of recent excavations. This rarity is even more striking because the houses excavated in Herculaneum by American archaeologists retained, by contrast, all their smaller objects. And yet the two cities were both victims of the same eruption. Many other countries have experienced what could be called 'bargain-offer' excavations. But in Pompeii, this exceptional site, the disappearance of objects seems to have reached a worrying level. There is practically nothing left that could be carried away in a pocket or a bag. The authorities have even had to give up leaving copies of antique objects (casts and false bronzes), let alone any original furniture in place, which would have constituted an exceptional history lesson for visitors.

Sometimes the restoration work itself is destructive

'Obviously,' says Jean-Pierre Adam, 'the archaeologists and authorities do not know what is happening, and even if they did, there is precious little they could do about it. You must remember that we are not far from Naples. Furthermore, the managers of the site are virtually obliged to employ local firms to carry out restoration work on Pompeii. These firms, who may be quite well versed in current building techniques, are completely incompetent when it comes

to matters of restoration.' Restoration work requires scrupulous care and extensive knowledge of specialized techniques. These conditions are not always met. And so, paradoxically, we see the restoration work hastening the deterioration it was intended to prevent.

Sometimes it is the fault of ancient work; they did not know any better. Perhaps they were not aware that lintels over window and door openings should be replaced with hard wood suitably seasoned to prevent rot and mould. Soft wood, insufficiently treated, quickly succumbs to attack; wood-eating insects move in, with disastrous consequences. Some mistakes are notorious: in the House of Meleager, in the north-west of the city, the roof timbers for a room 5 m x 11 m, designed to support the weight of over 5 tons of tiles, were erected with no triangular sections to give it strength; in spite of attempts to reinforce the roof with steel, the structure collapsed.

Blunders in the use of modern materials

Sadly, the reinforced concrete used on the site was often, according to the report's findings, 'particularly badly mixed'. Was this the result of repeated mistakes or of small savings on the cost of the materials? The concrete flakes away; the steel skeleton, exposed to the air, begins to rust and to expand, hastening the destruction of the building. Similar faults can be found in many of the mortar coatings applied to protect areas of ancient masonry. The poor quality mortar, which contains too much sand, tends to crack as it ages; soon water and vegetation start to penetrate.

This same uncertain mixture of incompetence and roguery can be seen in the restoration of painted plaster wall surfaces. The workmen of ancient times

used iron ties to attach the surface layers to the masonry behind them, but not only are these ugly, they also rust, expanding and cracking the plaster all round them. Yet more modern alternatives are scarcely any better.

To reattach the plaster to the masonry without having to remove it completely, they start by removing the crumbling edges from the surface that is to be consolidated. They then remove the old mortar using an iron rod poked up from below between the facing and its support. The gap is refilled with a liquid concrete poured down into the gap from above. Problems arise from the fact that the removal of the old mortar can never be complete. If it were, the whole surface would disintegrate, in spite of the supporting struts. So they leave some in place, which means that after the pouring process, there are two different types of mortar next to each other; being of a different composition, they react in different ways, causing cracks to form. This has resulted in the collapse of whole areas of wall surface.

The new mortar does not even fill the entire space. Investigations were carried out on a painted wall in the House of the Pygmies, restored in 1979; the height of the area being treated was 1.5 m, but the new liquid mortar ran down at best only 22 cm, and at worst, a mere 4 cm. The flows of plaster were not even contiguous. In addition, the load-bearing masonry was not treated in any way, so after a short time they had to repeat the process all over again. Once more, they had to scratch away at the edges of the top layer of plaster, and so on, until the whole thing had disappeared.

Clearly, the work of the 1st-century builders of Pompeii does not always help the 20th-century restorers. Analyses carried out in Paris show that, even where the plaster surfaces were executed with great care, what lay behind them was not necessarily of the same quality. The lime content of the mortar was often rather low, and this antique mortar, originally designed to save money, crumbles easily. It can even be eroded by the wind. In damp areas, it encourages

rising damp, which damages the painted murals. It is the difference in lime content between the wall and its covering that causes so many plaster surfaces to become detached. And finally, in the rubble of the wall itself, a variety of different materials was often used.

The fertility of the region is another enemy of the ruins

Farmers have always prized the land around Mount Vesuvius, because the soil there is some of the most fertile in the world. Several metres thick, the topsoil abounds in rapidly absorbed mineral salts, thanks to Vesuvius. In the time of Augustus, at the beginning of the 1st century AD, the geographer Strabo wrote that, in certain parts of Campania, you could get two wheat harvests, a third of millet, and sometimes even a fourth of vegetables. Even today, farmers in the region grow several crops of early vegetables, even planting them in the orchards. The same rich soil, only in a thinner layer, lies beneath Pompeii. The result is catastrophic.

Thirty-one parasitic plant varieties have been identified on the site by G. Aymonin of the National Museum for Natural History. There is a whole collection of weeds, from acanthus to wild carrot, from the fiercesome fennel and dreadful fig, to bindweed and brambles. First, the plants invade patches of bare earth. In the areas visited by tourists, the battle against the weeds is relatively easy, as the visitors' feet now become our allies. But in the houses that are closed to the public, enclosed areas of bare soil – in the peristyles, gardens, atria – are rapidly covered with a dense mat of vegetation, which soon reaches out towards the surrounding walls and attacks them. This is a particular problem in the most badly ruined houses close to the sectors that have not yet been excavated.

Vegetation also attacks concrete floors and their decoration. It can utterly destroy mosaic floors. As soon as a single one of the tiny cubes goes missing, a plant will come and take root there. It is even possible for the roots of plants

outside to force off the revetments. Most visitors are blissfully unaware of all this. They see no more than five or six houses, all of which are well kept, and remain quite oblivious of what is quietly being destroyed elsewhere. For the travelling exhibition on Pompeii that toured Europe recently, a plan was drawn up showing the areas of flooring in the excavated portion of the city that still have their original stone or marble coverings. They now constitute only a very small percentage of the total surface area. Yet when they were first excavated, they were all covered, every single one – with mortar in the case of the more humble dwellings, and with mosaics in the case of the richest. Thousands of square metres of floor covering must have disintegrated and simply ceased to exist. And the destruction continues.

Stonework may also be destroyed, when the covering has disappeared and the facing has been damaged or fallen away. On the tops of walls, brambles, fennel and broom take hold, soon forming a great mass of vegetation that results in falling masonry. Along the inside walls, valerian and brambles cling to the surfaces and dig their roots into the stonework, working their way under the facings. The roots grow, thicken, burying themselves ever more deeply. Cracks open up, also allowing damp to enter. Ivy, too, plays its part; it clings to the facings and weighs on them, encouraging them to come away. It is attached to the facing more tightly than the facing is attached to the wall, so when people try to remove the ivy, the whole surface of the wall comes away with it.

An archaeological disaster of the first order

Of course, all it would take is a small army of careful and dedicated cleaners to take up arms against these plagues. Plus a team of expert restorers.... Today, in the parts of Pompeii that are still closed to the public, you will find walls buried under a mass of vegetation, fissured masonry and cracked columns, crumbling mosaics in which one piece after another is falling away; invading plants, combined with damp, human damage and neglect, are threatening the site as much as the instability of the ground upon which it stands. There are houses which have been excavated, but which you can no longer enter because of the weeds growing there. Close to the unexcavated areas, some courtyards of the ancient houses have been transformed into jungles, which, left to their own devices, attack, crack and destroy at will.

It is a slow, gradual tragedy that will leave not a wrack behind. Pompeii has become the sorry example of how not to proceed in matters of restoration. It is a major archaeological disaster.

Henri de Saint-Blanquat
Science et Avenir, no. 469, March 1986

An archaeological itinerary

Although Pompeii is one of the best archaeological sites in the world, any visitor to the region should not miss the many important sites nearby, including especially those shown here.

With its patrician villas looking out over the sea, its impressive public monuments and its mild climate, Herculaneum rivalled the neighbouring city of Pompeii.

Stabiae, with its villas and baths, lay a few kilometres south of Pompeii; it was buried by the lava that flowed from Vesuvius in August AD 79.

Oplontis, which experts agree was located on the site of the present-day port of Torre Annunziata, has provided us with one of the finest suburban houses, the villa of Sabina Poppaea.

In antiquity, Boscoreale, on the slopes of Vesuvius above Pompeii, was made up of several farming estates and their villas; in one of these a fabulous silver treasure was discovered.

GLOSSARY

aedile Town magistrate who supervised the day-to-day administration of the city, such as maintaining order and repairing streets

ala (pl. **alae**) Side wing, opening to right or left at the far end of an atrium

amphora Two-handled vessel for liquids, especially wine, usually made of clay

apochae Receipts issued by a creditor, acknowledging payment of debt

apodyterium Changing or undressing room at the baths

atlantes Supports in the form of carved male figures

augustales Group of freedmen who celebrated the cult of the emperor, instituted by Tiberius in honour of Augustus

basilica Colonnaded public hall on the forum, used for commercial transactions and the dispensing of justice

caldarium Hot room in the baths

carcer (pl. **carceres**) Underground room at the amphitheatre where gladiators and wild beasts waited their turn

cardo Road from north to south

cavea, ima, media, summa Lower, middle and top sections of tiered seating in the theatre or amphitheatre

cella Main body of a classical temple, housing the cult statue

comitium Meeting place on the forum where magistrates assembled for voting

compluvium Square central opening in the roof over the domestic atrium

curia Senate house on the forum, where the decurion council met

decumanus Road from east to west

decurio (pl. **decuriones**) Councillors, often former magistrates

dolium (pl. **dolia**) Large earthenware jar, globular in form, with a wide mouth

duovir (pl. **duoviri**) Two senior magistrates of a colony, elected annually by the whole plebiscite, who presided over the decurion council and had law-giving powers

frigidarium Cold room at the baths

fullonica Fulling works or tannery

garum Fish sauce

Herm Name derived from early Greek statues of Hermes in the form of a rectangular shaft with a carved head. Later, they could carry the heads of other divinities

horti pompeiani Suburban market gardens of Pompeii

impluvium Pool in the centre of an atrium, immediately below the *compluvium* (see above)

insula Block of town houses

lararium Household shrine dedicated to the *lares*

lares Tutelary deities, originally from Etruscan religion, worshipped as the protectors of a particular locality. Most common are the *lares familiares* or *domestici*, the household gods; *lares compitales* gods of the crossroads

lictor (pl. **lictores**) Freeborn attendant granted to a magistrate as a sign of official dignity

ludus (pl. **ludi**) Public games or spectacles

macellum Market

magister (pl. **magistri**) Magistrates; *magistri vici et compiti* magistrates of the quarter and of the crossroads

monopteros Temple consisting of a single row of columns supporting a roof

oecus Richly decorated salon or drawing room

palaestra Sports ground, from the Greek for a wrestling school

patera Broad, flat dish or saucer used especially for offerings

peristyle Inner courtyard surrounded by a colonnade, of Hellenistic inspiration

podium Raised base of a temple, or parapet wall around the first row of seats at the amphitheatre

Priapus Rustic god of fertility, often portrayed with a huge penis

res publica Public service

retiarius Type of gladiator, net-fighter

sistrum Metallic rattle used in religious ceremonies

strigil Scraper made of horn or metal used by bathers to remove impurities from the skin

tablinum Central room at the far end of the atrium, often used as the main reception room

tabulae ceratae Wax-covered wooden tablets used for writing

tepidarium Warm room in the baths

thermopolium Tavern or bar serving warm drinks

tholos Beehive-shaped chamber built of stone

thyrsus Long staff entwined with ivy and vine leaves, and often tipped with a pine cone, carried by Dionysos and his followers

triclinium Dining room in a Roman house, or in the open air

uraeus Egyptian cobra sacred to Isis

velum Canopy suspended over the seats at a theatre or amphitheatre

venatio Hunting or the combat of wild beasts

vicini Inhabitants of a quarter, neighbours

vicomagister Freedman responsible for the cult of the *lares compitales* (see *lares* and *magister* above), from *vicus*, quarter

FURTHER READING

BACKGROUND TITLES

Bianchi Bandinelli, Ranuccio. *Rome: The Centre of Power. Roman Art to AD 200.* 1970
Boethius, Axel, and John B. Ward-Perkins. *Etruscan and Roman Architecture.* 1970
McKay, Alexander G. *Greek and Roman Domestic Architecture.* 1972
Salmon, Edward T. *Samnium and the Samnites.* 1967

GENERAL WORKS ON POMPEII AND HERCULANEUM

Brion, Marcel. *Pompeii and Herculaneum: The Glory and the Grief.* 1960
van Buren, A.W. *A Companion to the Study of Pompeii and Herculaneum.* 2nd ed. 1938
Carrington, Richard. *Pompeii.* 1936
Corti, Egon C. *The Destruction and Resurrection of Pompeii and Herculaneum.* 6th ed. 1951
Deiss, Joseph J. *Herculaneum, Italy's buried treasure.* 1966
de Franciscis, Alfonso. *The Buried Cities: Pompeii and Herculaneum.* 1978
Jashemski, Stanley A. and Wilhelmina F. *Pompeii.* 1965
Kraus, Theodor, and Leonard. von Matt. *Pompeii and Herculaneum: the Living Cities of the Dead.* 1975
Leppmann, Wolfgang. *Pompeii in Fact and Fiction.* 1968
Maiuri, Amedeo. *Herculaneum and the Villa of the Papyri.* 1963; *Pompeii.* 14th ed. 1970
Seaford, Richard. *Pompeii.* 1978
Ward-Perkins, John B., and Amanda Claridge. *Pompeii AD 79.* Royal Academy of Arts, London. 1976-7

DAILY LIFE IN THE SHADOW OF VESUVIUS

d'Arms, John H. *Romans on the Bay of Naples.* 1970
d'Avino, M. *The Women of Pompeii.* 1967
Castrén, Paavo. *Ordo Populusque Pompeianus, Polity and Society in Roman Pompeii.* 1975
Franklin, James L. *Pompeii. The Electoral Programmata, Campaigns and Politics 71-79.* 1980
Grant, Michael. *Cities of Vesuvius.* 1971
Jashemski, Wilhelmina F. *The Gardens of Pompeii, Herculaneum and the Villas Destroyed by Vesuvius.* 1979
Tanzer, Helen H. *The Common People of Pompeii.* 1939
Trevelyan, Raleigh. *The Shadow of Vesuvius:* 1976

ART AND ARCHITECTURE

Dwyer, Eugene J. *Pompeian Domestic Sculpture.* 1982
Gabriel, M. *Masters of Campanian Painting.* 1952
Gell, William, and John P. Gandi. *Pompeiana: the topography, edifices and ornaments of Pompeii,* 2 vols. 1817-19
Grant, Michael. *Erotic Art in Pompeii.* 1975
Mau, August. *Pompeii, its Life and Art* (transl. F.W. Kelsey). 1899

LIST OF ILLUSTRATIONS

The following abbreviations have been used: *a* above, *b* below, *c* centre, *l* left, *r* right.

COVER

INTRODUCTION

CHAPTER 1

199*l* Fourth Style mural in Pompeii partially destroyed by rising damp
199*r* The ravages of vegetation: a valerian plant causes cracking in a section of marble facing, Region VI
200 Graffiti on a wall in the House of Loreius
202*l* A house swamped by plants in Region VI

202*r* Collapse of a building in Region VII caused by the earthquake of 1980
203 Weeds take over at the edges of the excavations in Region III
204*a* and 205 Props support buildings in the streets of Pompeii
204*b* Tourists in Pompeii

INDEX

ACKNOWLEDGMENTS

We wish to thank the following: Mrs Bonaiutti of the Centre Jean-Bérard, Naples; Claude Albore-Livadie, researcher, CNRS, Naples; The Pagliara Foundation, University Institute Suor Orsola Benincasa, Naples; Jean-Pierre Adam, Dept of Classical Architecture, Vincennes; Gilles Sauron of the University of Dijon; Mrs Samson, head of photographic services, Bibliothèque Nationale, Paris; Claude Moatti, historian; Editions Grasset; the reviews *Archeologia* and *Science et Avenir*. Seneca, *Naturales Questiones,* vols VII and X, transl. by T. H. Corcoran, Harvard University Press, Cambridge, Mass., 1971, reprinted by permission of the publishers and the Loeb Classical Library; *Letters of the Younger Pliny,* transl. © B. Radice, 1963 (Penguin Classics, 1969), reproduced by permission of Penguin Books Ltd; Goethe, *Italian Journey,* transl. W.H. Auden and E. Mayer, © 1962 Pantheon Books, reprinted by permission of Harper Collins and Curtis Brown, Ltd; Stendhal, *Rome, Naples and Florence,* transl. Richard N. Coe, © John Calder (Publishers) Ltd, 1959, reprinted by permission of the Calder Educational Trust, London. Map and line drawings: Patrick Mérienne 46-7, 186.

PHOTO CREDITS

Jean-Pierre Adam, Paris 198-203, 205. Archiv für Kunst und Geschichte, Berlin 19*b*, 28-9, 48, 51, 61, 163, 170, 173. Artephot/Held, Paris 72*r*, 115. Artephot/Mandel, Paris 116. Artephot/Nimatallah, Paris 83, 126, 129. Artephot/Percheron, Paris 64*c*. Artephot/Ziolo, Paris 128. Didier Baussy, Paris 17*a* and *b*, 49*b*, 59*b*, 142. Bibliothèque de l'Institut, Paris 147. Bibliothèque Nationale, Paris 19*a*, 22*a* and *b*, 24, 25, 26-7, 52-3*a*, 65, 86-7, 88*b*, 99*a* and *b*, 103*a* and *b*, 107*a*, 110-11, 117, 135, 136, 143, 146, 149, 150-1. M.E. Boucher, Boulogne 43, 49*c*, 59*a*. Bulloz, Paris 55*a*, 56-7*a*, 82. Chuzeville, Paris 93, 107*b*, 111*b*, 192-7. Dagli-Orti, Paris 69b, 77, 78*br*, 91, 102, 112, 131. Dieuzaide, Toulouse 12-13. D.R. 44, 79, 106*a*, 128*b*, 130*b*, 138, 139*b*, 152, 159, 167, 202*a*. Edimédia, Paris 141. ENSBA, Paris *32–3*, page after p. 33, foldout 1, 35, 36-7*a* and *b*, 42, 74, 97*b*, foldout 2, page before p. 104, *104–5*. Explorer/Krafft, Paris 11. Giraudon, Paris 14-15, 66, 113. Hubert Josse, Paris 10. Magnum/Lessing, Paris 49*a*, 69*a*, 97, 98, 118*a*, 124. Musée de l'Assistance Publique, Paris 144. Nasjonalgalleriet, Oslo 45. National Trust, London 20-1. Rapho, Paris 202*b*. Rapho/Lawson 125. Rapho/Tholy 97. Rapho/Von Matt 64*b*, 185. RMN, Paris 100-1. Robert Etienne, Bordeaux 74-5*a*, 74*b*, 80, 81*a* and *b*, 88*a*, 94. Roger-Viollet, Paris 30a and b, 31, 39, 40, 56-7b, 60a, 63, 70, 71a, 72l, 73, 76, 78a, 94b, 118b, 119, 134, 139a, 140, 153-4, 157, 158, 160, 161, 166, 178, 179, 180. Rotondo, Naples 18, 24, 41, 148, 155, 182. Jean Roubier, Paris 60*c*. Scala, Florence 54, 67, 84-5, 90, 92, 114, 120-3, 127, 130, 186-91. Société de Géographie, Paris 168-9. Victoria and Albert Museum, London 132-3. U.D.F., Paris 55*b*, 62, 89, 108-9. Werner Forman Archives, London 68.

Robert Etienne
discovered the enduring fascination of Pompeii in
1939, when he read F. Thédenat's study of the
city. He first visited Pompeii and studied its
wealth of archaeological material while a member
of the Ecole de Rome in 1948. In 1951 he was
commissioned to prepare a book on daily life in
Pompeii, and he twice stayed there during the
month of August, in order to relive the
anniversary of the dreadful catastrophe, on the
very spot where it had occurred. For the past
twenty-five years he has regularly returned there
for periods of study, and he shares the concern of
all those who are alarmed by the gradual decay
of this prestigious ancient city. Today Robert
Etienne is professor at the University of
Bordeaux.

For Emmanuelle and Véronique

Translated by Caroline Palmer

First published in the United Kingdom in 1997

by Thames & Hudson Ltd, 181A High Holborn,
London WC1V 7QX

Reprinted 1992, 1994, 1998, 2002

English translation © 1992 Thames & Hudson Ltd
London, and Harry N. Abrams, Inc., New York,

© Gallimard 1986

British Library Cataloguing-in-Publication Data

A catalogue record for this book is available
from the British Library

ISBN 0–500–30011–9

Printed and bound in Italy
by Editoriale Lloyd, Trieste